Vocabulary Escapades

Dynamic Learning Adventures

I'M STOCKPILING WORDS!

plethora
irascible
inane
exuberant
ubiquitous
gourmand
escapade

by Marjorie Frank

Illustrated by Kathleen Bullock

Incentive Publications, Inc.
Nashville, Tennessee

To Teachers and Parents

- Use each vocabulary escapade as a short warm-up to motivate the enjoyment of words, OR use each escapade as the basis for a vocabulary lesson, OR focus on a particular vocabulary skill with a group of escapades that sharpen that skill.

- Use all the questions or tasks on a page, taking time to discuss each one, OR choose the tasks that fit your students' needs.

- Let students work alone or in pairs on the pages, OR use them with the whole group.

- Help students connect the words to their real lives. Engage them with each word in as many different ways as you can possibly concoct. USE, USE, USE the words in front of them.

- Help students connect the cartoons and comic strips to the words. Encourage them to create their own cartoons for showing meaning of these and other words.

- The words used in this book are taken from lists of words that show up on standardized tests (such as the pre-SAT, SAT, and ACT) as well as from well-researched vocabulary programs for middle school students. These are words students will encounter in their texts and wider culture.

- See pages 5-8 for lists of skills and standards supported by the escapades, 100-105 for a cumulative assessment, and 107-110 for an alphabetical list of the words with meanings and pronunciations.

Illustrated by Kathleen Bullock
Cover design by Debbie Weekly
Edited by Joy MacKenzie

ISBN 978-0-86530-525-0

1   2   3   4   5   6   7   8   9   10   14   13   12   11

Printed by Sheridan Books, Inc., Chelsea, Michigan • June 2011
www.incentivepublications.com

What do you get when you mix the antics of a clever, street-smart rat with a hundred enticing (and important) words? You gain a better vocabulary—plus a whole lot of adventuresome, brain-stretching fun!

Wonderful, Wonderful Words!

Join Rosco Rat and his band of fetching friends (all of whom, by the way, have astonishingly rich vocabularies) to learn words in a way you won't soon forget.

- You never know what escapade Rosco will stir up next!

- Each one connects words to imaginative situations.

- Each one invites you to deeply explore the meanings of one or more words, ignites your curiosity, and challenges you to use the word or words in many different ways.

- The book is full of surprises, humor, delightful cartoons, and intrigue. It will leave you with the gifts of greater word understanding, a broader vocabulary, and a lot more excitement about words.

CONTENTS

Appendix

To the Student:
Never Forget These Words!

REALLY . . . YOU WON'T FORGET THEM!

Here's how to use this book to make these words part of your vocabulary forever:

- Start every escapade by reading the word and its definition at the top of the page.

- Then read the cartoon or comic strip to see what the characters are doing. Take time to ponder and discuss the connection between the visual image and the word.

- Look up the word in your dictionary. Compare the definitions. Notice other definitions of the word.

- Answer the questions and do the tasks suggested on the page. This will help you fool around with the word in many different ways. This helps you to remember it!

- Think about where you have heard or read the word before.

- Think about other words you know that look or sound similar.

- Look hard at the word and try to take it apart. Pay attention to its root, and to any prefixes, suffixes, or endings.

- Look in a thesaurus to find synonyms and antonyms of the word.

- Make a list of places and situations where the word might be useful.

- Be on the lookout for the word at home, at school, and in conversations.

- When you hear of see one of these words used anywhere, show it or share it with others.

- Most of all . . . USE the word in many places, ways, and situations.

- Do other things with a word besides reading it or writing it . . .

Discuss it with someone else or teach it to someone.

Create a poster, rap, drama, slogan, or story around it.

Act it out. Sing it. Dance to it. Tap it. Chant it.

Draw the word or draw something about it.

Vocabulary Standards and Skills Supported by the Escapades

Skill	Escapade Number(s)
Learn and use new words	all escapades
Find the meaning of an unknown word	all escapades
Use a newly-learned word in a variety of situations	all escapades
Associate a word with a visual image	all escapades
Use humor to strengthen word meaning	all escapades
Use a word in various forms (different tenses, endings, parts of speech, etc.)	all escapades
Use context clues to determine a word's meaning	3, 4, 7, 9,12, 13, 14, 18, 22, 23, 24, 26, 28, 31, 32, 34, 35, 37, 40, 41, 54, 55, 60, 64, 68, 72, 75
Relate word meaning to meanings of word parts (roots, prefixes, suffixes, endings)	3, 4, 5, 11, 17, 19, 20, 26, 31, 35, 40, 62, 69, 76, 78, 81
Find, recognize, or compare synonyms of a word	2, 5, 7, 22, 27, 28, 31, 32, 40, 42, 44, 55, 59, 63, 80, 81
Find, recognize, or compare antonyms of a word	5, 9, 10, 27, 28, 31, 42, 44, 55, 62, 82, 83, 84
Explore and explain a word's connotation	31, 53, 61, 67, 71, 85
Identify, define, and use multiple meanings of a word	6, 8, 9, 11, 12, 14, 16, 17, 19, 20, 21, 24, 26, 29, 41, 46, 48, 50, 52, 55, 56, 61, 62, 66, 70, 77, 78, 81, 86, 89
Distinguish among words that are easily confused with each other	3, 6, 11, 20, 26, 29, 30, 34, 35, 38, 45, 48, 49, 55, 57, 60, 64, 70, 72, 80, 82, 86
Develop mnemonic techniques to remember word meaning	21, 22, 25, 45, 47, 54, 71, 84
Identify words that are associated with one another	6, 7, 11, 12, 16, 17, 20, 29, 30, 31, 32, 33, 34, 35, 38, 40, 48, 49, 60, 70, 73, 80, 81, 82, 86
Choose appropriate words to complete analogies	10, 43, 51, 69, 83, 84
Create a visual image to demonstrate word meaning	2, 3, 11, 12, 16, 17, 21, 28, 39, 40, 42, 52, 54, 55, 60, 66, 67, 75, 77, 78, 81, 87, 89
Use movement or action to demonstrate a word	8, 12, 13, 38, 49, 63, 65, 77, 87
Show understanding of word meaning through completion of a writing task	1, 4, 9, 12, 15, 18, 22, 32, 47, 51, 57, 59, 67, 72, 73, 75, 78, 82, 86, 87, 88
Examine causes, effects, examples, nonexamples, or implications of the idea, concept, or action named by a word	all escapades
Make personal and real-life connections to a word	all escapades
Connect a word to previous knowledge of a similar word or of the concept named by the word	all escapades
Make judgments based on understanding of a word's meaning	all escapades

Common Core Standards Supported by the Escapades

Anchor Standards for	Number and Category	Standard
Reading	**4:** Craft and Structure	Interpret words and phrases as they are used in a text, including determining technical, connotative, and figurative meanings, and analyze how specific word choices shape meaning or tone.
Speaking and Listening	**2:** Comprehension and Collaboration	Integrate and evaluate information presented in diverse media and formats, including visually, quantitatively, and orally.
Language	**4:** Vocabulary Acquisition and Use	Determine or clarify the meaning of unknown and multiple-meaning words and phrases by using context clues, analyzing meaningful word parts, and consulting general and specialized reference materials, as appropriate.
Language	**5:** Vocabulary Acquisition and Use	Demonstrate understanding of word relationships and nuances in word meanings.

Thinking Skills Supported by the Escapades
Structure Based on Bloom's Taxonomy of Cognitive Development

Cognitive Domain Levels *Simplest ⟶ Most Complex*	Skills	Escapade Number(s)
Remembering: Recall data or information	arrange, define, describe, duplicate, label, list, match, name, order, recall, recognize, repeat, reproduce, select, state	Escapades 1-90
Understanding: Understand the meaning, translation, interpolation, and interpretation of instructions and problems. Explain concepts and state a problem in one's own words	classify, describe, discuss, explain, express, identify, indicate, locate, recognize, report, select, translate, paraphrase	Escapades 1-90
Applying: Use a concept in a new situation or unprompted use of an abstraction	apply, choose, demonstrate, dramatize, employ, illustrate, interpret, operate, practice, schedule, sketch, solve, use, write	Escapades 1-90
Analyzing: Distinguish among component parts to arrive at meaning or understanding	analyze, appraise, calculate, categorize, compare, contrast, criticize, differentiate, discriminate, distinguish, examine, experiment, question, test	Escapades 1-90
Evaluating: Justify a decision or position; make judgments about the value of an idea	appraise, argue, assess, defend, evaluate, judge, rate, select, support, value, compose, construct, create, design, develop, formulate, manage, organize, plan, set up, prepare, propose, write	Escapades 1-90
Creating: Create a new product or viewpoint	assemble, construct, create, design, develop, formulate, mold, prepare, propose, synthesize, write	Escapades 1, 2, 3, 4, 5, 7, 11, 12, 13, 15, 16, 17, 21, 24, 28, 29, 30, 36, 39, 40, 42, 49, 51, 52, 53, 54, 55, 60, 63, 66, 67, 71, 72, 74, 76, 78, 81, 85, 78, 88, 89, 89

Learning Vocabulary the Brain-Compatible Way

Most of us can learn a list of words for a test. But you don't really KNOW a word until it becomes comfortable—a normal part of your everyday vocabulary.

Brain-compatible learning theory is based on information that neuroscientists have learned about how the brain perceives, senses, processes, stores, and retrieves information. Brain-based learning principles offer useful strategies for learning vocabulary in ways that cement understanding and fix the words in long-term memory.

You are most likely to remember a new word if . . .

- it is connected to art, visuals, graphics, cartoons, or color.

- humor is used in presenting and explaining the word.

- music or rhythm are connected to the learning of the word.

- your WHOLE body is involved in the learning.

- you DO something to actively demonstrate the word.

- the word is connected to or learned in the context of a strong emotion.

- you get involved with the word and give feedback about it.

- you use the word in a variety of forms and ways.

- the word is connected to real-life experiences.

- you connect the word to other situations and words that you already know.

- you see it, read it, hear it, look for it, and listen to it many times.

- the word is presented in a context that is sensible and relevant.

- the word is taken apart so that you understand its root and affixes.

- you discuss, share, use, explain, and demonstrate the word with other people.

- you develop (or are taught) a mnemonic device (memory trick) to help you remember the word.

- you think about and write or discuss the causes, results, examples, and nonexamples of the idea named by the word.

- it is learned in an environment that is relatively free from stress and threat.

escapade

(n) an unconventional adventure

1. An *escapade* is an adventure that runs counter to accepted behavior. What is unconventional about Rosco's *escapade*?

2. Think of an escapade that might take place in each of the locations shown with the letters of the word *escapade*. Write a phrase to describe the adventure. (Do not suggest any adventures that are illegal or hurtful to people involved.)

Escalator_____

Science lab_____

Cafeteria_____

Amusement park_____

Park_____

Alley or avenue_____

Dinner table_____

Entertainment center_____
(such as a theater)

3. What is the most memorable *escapade* of your life? If you had it to do over again, would you repeat it? Write a brief description of the *escapade*. Tell why you would (or wouldn't) do it again.

Name_____

gourmand

(n) one who is excessively fond of eating and drinking good food

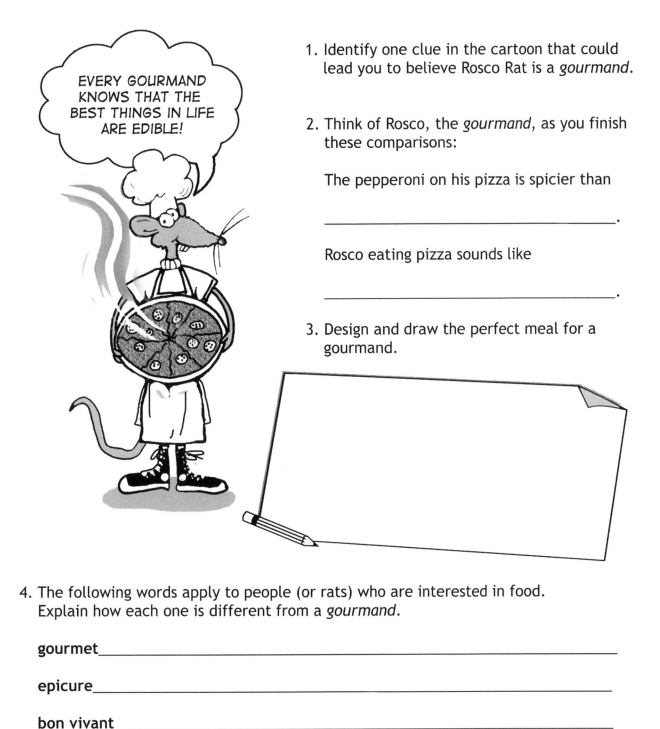

EVERY GOURMAND KNOWS THAT THE BEST THINGS IN LIFE ARE EDIBLE!

1. Identify one clue in the cartoon that could lead you to believe Rosco Rat is a *gourmand*.

2. Think of Rosco, the *gourmand*, as you finish these comparisons:

   The pepperoni on his pizza is spicier than

   _____.

   Rosco eating pizza sounds like

   _____.

3. Design and draw the perfect meal for a gourmand.

4. The following words apply to people (or rats) who are interested in food. Explain how each one is different from a *gourmand*.

   gourmet_____

   epicure_____

   bon vivant _____

Name_____

indolent

(adj) averse to activity, effort, or movement; habitually lazy

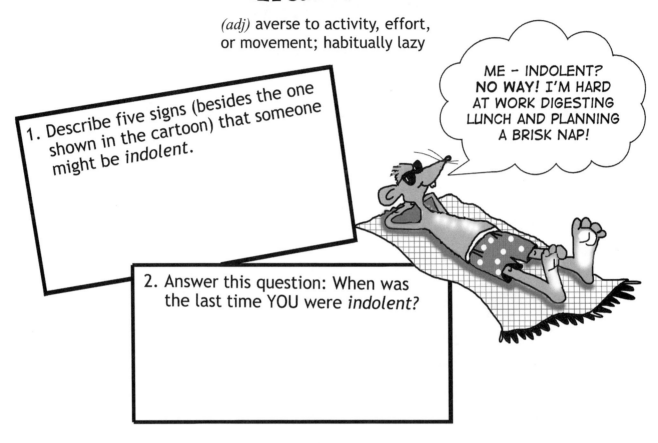

1. Describe five signs (besides the one shown in the cartoon) that someone might be *indolent*.

2. Answer this question: When was the last time YOU were *indolent*?

ME – INDOLENT? NO WAY! I'M HARD AT WORK DIGESTING LUNCH AND PLANNING A BRISK NAP!

3. Create a name for an *indolent* character in a cartoon. _____

4. Teach someone the meaning of the word *indolent*. Do this by writing a sentence that conveys the meaning without giving the definition.

5. Circle the root of the word *indolent*.

Another word that has the same root is *doldrums*. Find out what this word means. Draw a picture of someone or something that's "in the doldrums."

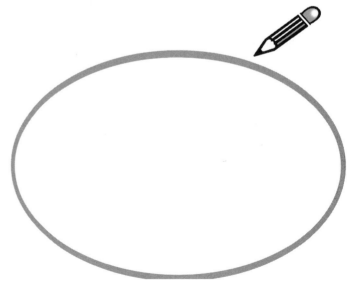

Name_____

concise

(adj) brief and to the point: succinct

BOOMERANG, MAKE A CONCISE LIST OF YOUR FAVORITE DESSERTS.

OKEY-DOKEY.

1. What do you notice about the use of the word *concise* in the cartoon?

2. Proverbs are *concise* statements of important ideas or advice. Each of the following is a *not-so-concise* version of a common English proverb. Identify the *concise* saying OR write your own *concise* version of the idea.

   a. The fluffy tiger-striped feline pet prematurely reached mortality due to her unrelenting, intense inquisitiveness.

   b. It is not only improbable but also impossible that you would be able to succeed at instructing a geriatric canine in a contemporary version of a deception or duplicity.

3. The word *concise* has the same root as the word *scissors*. Explain what you think the words have in common.

4. Read the poem. Then make it *concise*. (Write a short summary of the main idea.)

   TO SERVE ME TEA, TAKE THIS ADVICE:
   FILL YOUR KETTLE (A GREAT DEVICE),
   GET THE BAGS AND BREW THEM TWICE,
   ADD SOME MINT, THEN STIR IT THRICE.
   POUR IT GENTLY OVER ICE.
   BAKE SOME PUDDING MADE WITH RICE
   AND APPLE PIE. (I'LL NEED A SLICE.)
   BRING IT NOW. AHHHH! THIS IS NICE!

Name_____

uninhibited

(adj) unself-conscious; free from restaint

1. An *inhibition* is some inner restraint that impedes (blocks) free expression or activity. Music helps Rosco Rat lose his *inhibitions*. What helps you to lose yours?

2. Name something that your *inhibitions* would NEVER allow you to do.

3. Label each word **S** if it has a similar meaning to *uninhibited* or **O** if it has a meaning opposite from *uninhibited*.

___spontaneous   ___daring

___unwary   ___cautious

___reserved   ___guarded

___impetuous   ___free-spirited

> THIS IS ROCKIN'!

4. For each example, tell what a person might do if he or she feels *uninhibited* in the situation.

SINGING IN A CHOIR OR ROCK GROUP

MARCHING IN A BAND

GIVING A SPEECH

LISTENING TO A ROUSING SPEECH

Name_____

pretense

(n) the act of pretending; a false appearance or action intended to deceive

1. Why might someone claim that Boomerang Cat's statement is a *pretense*?

2. Describe how someone might act if he or she were making a *pretense* of being sick.

3. Fill in the blanks to finish the statements with behaviors you've seen or done.

a. I've watched_____ make a *pretense*
   (a person or character from a book or movie)

of being _____.

b. I, myself, have been known to make a *pretense* of_____.

---

4. A *pretense* is a false message, that sometimes (but not always) has an element of showiness. Rank these actions in order according to the *pretentiousness*, with #1 being the most *pretentious* (in your opinion).

_____ dressing up as a dog and sneaking into a dog show

_____ trying to lure a rich boyfriend by driving an expensive, borrowed car

_____ acting as if you understand the algebra lesson when you don't

_____ constantly telling your friends that you're okay, when something really terrible is going on in your life

_____ carrying a stack of books home every night to give your parents the impression you are a serious student (when you are not)

Name_____

culpable

(adj) liable; responsible; at fault

GUILTY AS CHARGED! WHAT GAVE ME AWAY?

1. Circle the word in Rosco's talk bubble that is a **synonym** for *culpable*.

2. Identify or describe the person (or other character) who might be *culpable* for each of these situations.

HOLES ALL OVER THE BACK YARD

SOGGY NEWSPAPERS ON THE FRONT LAWN

AN EMPTY GAS TANK IN THE FAMILY CAR

CHOCOLATE-Y FINGERPRINTS IN THE HALLWAY

SLOPPY NOSE-PRINTS ON THE WINDOW

ALL THE COOKIES GONE FROM THE COOKIE JAR

A SERIES OF UN-DONE HOMEWORK ASSIGNMENTS

3. *Culpability* is not just about being liable for a crime. There are many things for which someone may be *culpable*. Name at least two actions or incidents for which you have been *culpable*.

_____

_____

4. A *culprit* is one who is *culpable* for an incident.

   a. Who might be the *culprit* in this scene?

   b. For what is the *culprit culpable*?

Name

synchronize

(v) occur at the same time; to operate in unison

1. How does the comic strip show that Boomerang's friendship is *synchronized* with Rosco's?

2. Name two *synchronized* occurrences you have seen recently.

3. Stop and *synchronize* watches or other timekeeping devices with your classmates or others around you. Write the *synchronized* time:

   _____

4. Do another short *synchronized* activity right now. What did you do?

5. The popular expression *in sync* comes from the word *synchrony*. It is used to describe things or people that go together well or "hit it off." Which of the following would you describe as being *in sync*? (Mark them with an **X**.)

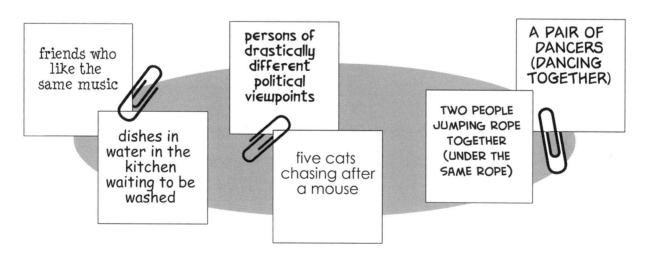

Name_____

unabashed

(adj) not ashamed; not embarrassed; not surprised

1. Read the talk bubbles. Find out what *ardor* means. Then name someone or something for which you have *unabashed ardor*.

> APPARENTLY, BOOMERANG'S ARDOR FOR PORTIA IS UNABASHED!

> I HATE FLOWERS. THEY MAKE ME SNEEZE.

UNBRIDLED   HUMILIATED   **haughty**   EGOTISTICAL

bashful   **CONFIDENT**

AGHAST   brazen   embarrassed

audacious   astonished   **chagrined**   flaunting

ASHAMED   modest   nonplussed

self-conscious

2. Draw a line connecting words that could be **antonyms** for *unabashed*. Have a dictionary handy to help with words you do not know.

3. Describe a behavior or situation that might cause you to be *abashed* rather than *unabashed*.

Name_____

virtuous

(adj) pure; morally good; righteous

nefarious

(adj) extremely wicked; evil

1. The cartoons show Rosco Rat playing the roles of two different kinds of characters. Explain how they communicate the opposite meanings of *nefarious* and *virtuous*.

2. What *nefarious* deed have you seen, heard about, or read about?

3. Where might you find some *nefarious* and *virtuous* characters or people in the same setting?

4. Finish the analogies by circling the correct word to fit in the blank.

      a. mischievous : nefarious :: _____ : crime

         vile   **punishment**   **prank**   **honorable**

      b. virtuous : nefarious : strict:_____

         lenient   **rigid**   **laudable**   **stingy**

      c. _____ : energetic :: noble : nefarious

         diligent   **indolent**   **patient**   **capable**

Name_____

incognito

(adv) with one's identity concealed; unknown

ARE WE TOO CONSPICUOUS?

1. Rosco often shows up with his identity concealed. What might be his reason for being *incognito* this time (as shown in the cartoon)?

2. List three reasons why someone might choose to attend an event or visit a location *incognito*.

   1 _____   2 _____

   3 _____

3. In the tale of "Little Red Riding Hood," a character operates *incognito*. What is that character's purpose for appearing *incognito*?

4. The root of *incognito* is *cog*, which means "know" or "known." Many other words have the same root. Here are some of them. Define two or more.

   COGNITION   COGENT   RECOGNIZE   INCOGNIZANT   COGITATE

5. Draw a picture of Rosco Rat, Boomerang Cat, or yourself *incognito*. Under the picture, write the place or occasion for the deception.

   Or, if you'd rather describe than draw, write a reason for being *incognito* and tell what you would do to appear that way.

Name_____

undulate

(v) rise and fall regularly;
move in a flowing motion

1. What might *undulate* as Boomerang
   pursues the activity in the cartoon?

2. Draw or design the word
   undulate in a way that
   shows what it means.
   Use only the letters of
   the word in your drawing.
   Fill the space.

3. Find the meaning of the word *fluctuate*. Which of these would be more likely to
   undulate than to *fluctuate?* (Circle one or more.)

   THE PRICE OF GASOLINE   YOUR FAVORITE SONG

   THE TRACK OF A ROLLERCOASTER

4. Answer these questions about *undulating* circumstances.

   a. When might you see a road undulate?

   b. What would you need to do to cause pudding to undulate?

   c. Where would you see an undulating surface?

   d. For what reason would you draw undulating lines?

Name_____

                                       Vocabulary Escapades—Learning Adventures Series

monotony

(n) tedious sameness

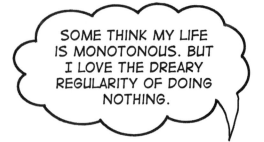

SOME THINK MY LIFE IS MONOTONOUS. BUT I LOVE THE DREARY REGULARITY OF DOING NOTHING.

1. Circle the phrase in Rosco's talk bubble that actually defines the word *monotony*.

2. Create a rhythm for the word *monotony*. Drum it on your desk repeatedly for 60 seconds. Make sure it sounds *monotonous*.

3. Read these words to yourself in a whisper. Repeat each one five times. Put an **X** by those that have a sound or rhythm so *monotonous* that they might just put you to sleep or bore you to distraction.

___ euphoria	___exponential	___ridiculous	___ frivolity
___ luscious	___telepathy	___conformity	___ frenzied
___ epiphany	___ elastic	___ retrograde	___ lasagna
___ serendipity	___ lugubrious	___ rigor	___ perpetual

Add a *monotonous* word to the above list. (Do not use *monotony* or any form of it).

My top 10 most monotonous things:

10 _____
9 _____
8 _____
7 _____
6 _____
5 _____
4 _____
3 _____
2 _____
1 _____

4. Write a **TOP 10** list of the most *monotonous* words, phrases, or situations that you have seen, heard, or experienced.

Name_____

negligible

(adj) so small or unimportant as to deserve little attention

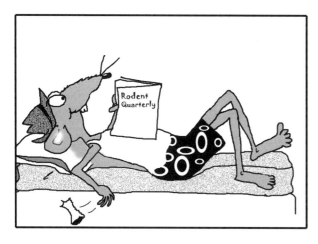

negligent

(adj) habitually disregarding; carelessly leaving something unattended

1. Describe the difference between *negligible* and *negligence* as shown in the two cartoons.

2. Identify at least two things that you possess in *negligible* amounts.

3. Sometimes *negligence* (being *negligent*) is against the law.
   Give an example of *negligence* that you believe is or should be illegal.

4. Are the words *negligible* and *negligent* used correctly below? Write *yes* or *no* for each sentence.

   _____a. The negligible amount of studying you did paid off with a failing grade.

   _____b. Todd hasn't been negligent in taking care of the lawn; it's just that the rainfall lately has been negligible.

   _____c. Her bank account has negligible funds because she's negligent about saving.

   _____d. I'm not negligible with clothing care. I paid extra for these wrinkled jeans!

Name_____

histrionics *(n)* deliberate show of emotion for effect

1. What do you imagine that Boomerang hopes to accomplish with these *histrionics*?

IT'S NOT FAIR!

2. Think of a person or character who has shown emotion for effect in a way that you would describe as *histrionics*. (You can include yourself.) Identify the situation in which this occurred.

3. The word *histrionics* has nothing to do with history. But, there probably have been and will continue to be many in history. Describe an example of *histrionics* that you think would be memorable enough to go down in history.

4. Think about the kinds of things a person might do or say when giving a showy display of emotion for effect. For each letter of the word *histrionics*, write a word or phrase to identify a behavior or expression.

H _____
i _____
S _____
T _____
R _____
i _____
O _____
N _____
i _____
C _____
S _____

Dear Boomerang,
I do not want to be
your girlfriend.
signed,

Portia

Name_____

dilemma

(n) undesirable choice; predicament

1. What, exactly, is Rosco Rat's *dilemma*?

2. How do you imagine Rosco will respond to the *dilemma*?

3. Explain how you would respond to the following *dilemma*:

You have been bestowed the honor of dining with the queen. The royal staff members have instructed you not to speak to the queen unless she speaks to you first. During dinner, the queen lifts a fork full of salad to her mouth. Alas, a large spider is perched atop the salad! You see it. The queen does not.

4. How is the word DILEMMA related to the word QUANDARY? (You may need to look up *quandary* in your dictionary.)

5. Try to remember your worst *dilemma*. Draw one or more images to show the choices you had or the predicament in which you find yourself.

Name_____

peril

(n) danger; exposure to the risk of being injured, destroyed, or lost

1. Rosco seems to be running for his life! Identify two different *perils* that he might be trying to avoid.

2. Briefly describe a *peril* you have avoided or hope to avoid.

3. Draw a *perilous* situation that might face Rosco. Label your drawing.

4. The table shows some meanings of word parts. Use the information to decide the meaning of each of these words. (Try to do this without consulting your dictionary.)

perish

perishable

imperil

perilous

Word Part	Kind of Part	Meaning(s)
per	root	destruction
able	suffix	capable of being
ish	suffix	like; become
il	suffix	go toward; capable of being; exposure to
im	prefix	cause to be
ous	suffix	like; pertaining to

Name_____

bamboozle

(v) deceive by underhanded methods; con

1. How do you think Rosco managed to *bamboozle* Boomerang into the situation shown in the cartoon?

2. What is the last thing you were *bamboozled* into doing or not doing?

3. How might someone *bamboozle* another person into eating ants?

4. *Bamboozle* is a word with ENERGY! This is the way one artist pictured it. Describe what you see that conveys the word's meaning or feeling.

Name_____

Vocabulary Escapades—Learning Adventures Series

incongruous

(adj) out of place in a situation; inappropriate

1. What makes the friendship of Rosco and Boomerang *incongruous*?

2. Which of these seem *incongruous* to you?
(Mark them with an X.)

___ someone meditating at a wrestling match

___ a mother ordering one scoop of
ice cream for a child who wants three

___ students studying in a library

___ lamb chops on a menu at a vegetarian convention

___ rattlesnakes at a petting zoo

___ a professional violinist claiming that her favorite music is hip-hop

___ rowdy behavior on a playground

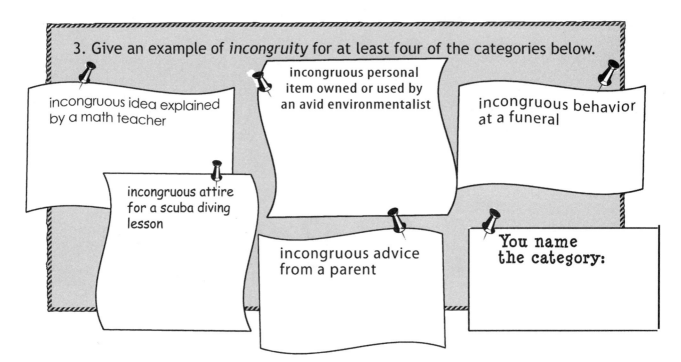

3. Give an example of *incongruity* for at least four of the categories below.

incongruous idea explained
by a math teacher

incongruous personal
item owned or used by
an avid environmentalist

incongruous behavior
at a funeral

incongruous attire
for a scuba diving
lesson

incongruous advice
from a parent

You name
the category:

Name_____

eminent

(adj) outstanding; utmost; well-known and respected

imminent

(adj) just about to happen

AS THE WORLD'S PREEMINENT SKATEBOARDER, ACCLAMATIONS FOR ME ARE IMMINENT!

IS THAT CHEERING I HEAR?

ROSCO ROCKS

1. The prefix *pre* means "most" or "first." So what does Rosco mean when he says that he is the *preeminent* skateboarder in the world?

2. Rosco also **hopes** that a cheese sandwich lunch is *imminent*. Name something that you hope is *imminent*.

Name something that you are **afraid** is *imminent*.

3. Write the name of someone who is *eminent* in each of these fields:

music _____

art _____

sports _____

leadership _____

acting _____

education _____

4. Mark sentences that use *imminent* correctly.

I have this terrible feeling that a science test is imminent.

A large, ferocious dog is approaching. I fear Rosco Rat is in imminent danger.

Even the bomb squad approaches an explosive device with imminent caution.

Robert Frost was an imminent poet.

Name_____

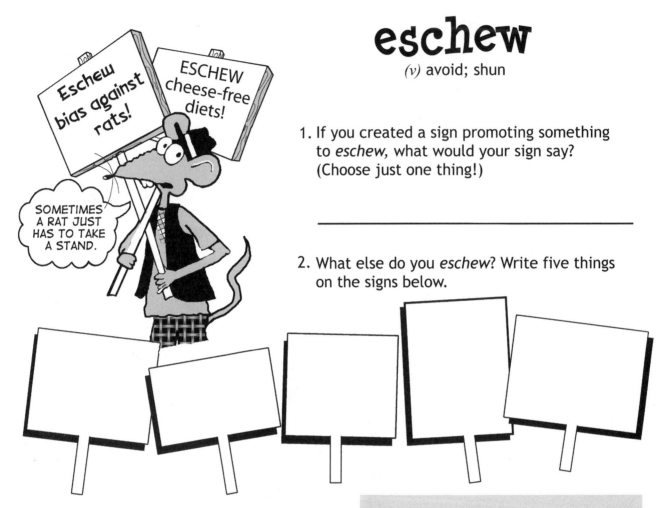

eschew
(v) avoid; shun

1. If you created a sign promoting something to *eschew,* what would your sign say? (Choose just one thing!)

_____

2. What else do you *eschew?* Write five things on the signs below.

3. The meaning of *eschew* has nothing to do with the word *chew.* But you can use the second word to help you remember the first. Use the word *chew* as you finish the poem.

   Cheese-free diets and
   Biases, too
   Are things our friend Rosco
   Would like to eschew.

   He thrives on excesses
   Of napping and stew
   Cheese pizzas, lasagna,

   _____

4. How important is it to you to *eschew* these things? Rank them in order, with 1 being the most crucial.

   ___ goo on your shoe

   ___ getting up in the morning

   ___ greasy food

   ___ being late

   ___ people who never stop texting

   ___ push-ups

   ___ gossip

   ___ cheating

   ___ bubblegum in your hair

   ___ rude behavior

Name_____

egregious

(adj) notably bad

1. What deed could Rosco do that would be the opposite of *egregious*?

2. Describe a time that you made or witnessed an *egregious* mistake.

3. Which words have meanings similar to *egregious*? (Circle them.)

GROSS   PICAYUNE

FLAGRANT   PETTY   INSIGNIFICANT

SHOCKING   PALTRY   MINOR

INSUFFERABLE   NOTORIOUS   HEINOUS

GRIEVOUS

4. Name or describe an *egregious* . . .

idea_____TV show_____

song_____decision_____

kind of food_____prospect for the future _____

behavior_____world event _____

public blunder_____

Name_____

coincidence

(n) the occurrence of events that happen at the same time by accident but seem to have a connection

1. Why does Rosco think that it is NOT a *coincidence* that his pal Boomerang always shows up at dinnertime?

WELL, I WAS IN THE NEIGHBORHOOD AND . . .

2. Many things *coincide* with one another (happen at the same time). Some of them happen at the same time because they are connected. (It's no *coincidence* that these happen.) For other occurrences, there is no connection, even if there seems to be. (These are pure *coincidence*.) Decide if each pair of simultaneous occurrences below is accidental or not. Draw a line connecting them to the right thought bubble.

COINCIDENCE

NOT A COINCIDENCE

a. A lady picks a 4-leaf clover. The same week, she finds her lost cat.

b. Rosco makes a $5 purchase of white cheddar at the *Cheese to Please Delicatessen* on 23rd Avenue the same day Boomerang drops a five dollar bill on the sidewalk.

c. Lucy is with her new boyfriend at a dressy dance party. Her mom's new rhinestone earrings are missing.

d. There is no school today. The mall is crowded with teenagers.

e. Thomas's middle name is Michael. At camp, he draws a name from a basket to select a bunkmate. The name he draws is of another kid named Thomas Michael.

Name_____

regalia

(n) symbols of royalty; finery befitting a king or royal figure

BRING MY JEWELS AND SCEPTER — PRONTO!

1. What *regalia* shows up in this cartoon?

2. Identify a situation in which you have seen *regalia*.

3. Which of these would be logical places to find *regalia*? (Circle them.)

at a costume party	in a courtroom	in a museum
on a pizza	inside a backpack	under a bridge
at a parade	in a photograph	on a history website
on a stage	on a subway	in a safe deposit box
in a closet	at a coronation	under a doghouse

4. Assume that by some stroke of fortune (or misfortune), you have landed in a position of royalty. What *regalia* would you possess, collect, or wear?

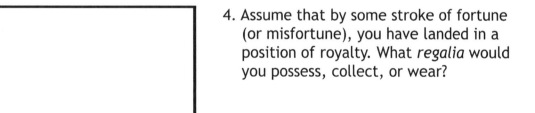

Name_____

ubiquitous

(adj) ever present; seemingly everywhere

1. What do you imagine Rosco and Boomerang will do about these *ubiquitous* spiders?

2. Name one *ubiquitous* thing or occurrence that you would most like to see reduced in your life.

3. What do you wish was *ubiquitous* in your life?

4. Find a word within the word *ubiquitous* that will help you remember the meaning. Circle that word and explain how you will use it to make sure you never forget what *ubiquitous* means.

5. Name something *ubiquitous* for each letter in the word.

Name_____

benign

(adj) gentle; not harmful;
not malignant

HOW COULD SOMETHING AS BENIGN AS A COMPLAINT ABOUT CAFETERIA FOOD SPARK SUCH DIRE CONSEQUENCES?

1. Is the action shown in the cartoon a *benign* activity? Why or why not?

2. What *benign* response could Rosco Rat make?

3. Each of the following sentences includes a word that contains the word part *bene* (meaning "good" or "well"). Circle the word and decide its meaning from the context of the sentence. Briefly explain the meaning.

   a. A mouse can run fast, change direction quickly, and squeeze into small spaces. These talents become benefits when she's being chased by an adoring cat.

   b. Street-wise and benevolent, Roscoe Rat shares his food finds with other hungry critters.

   c. Since Rosco is the only beneficiary named in Grandpa's will, he'll inherit the entire fortune (including Grandpa's prized cheese collection).

   d. The bakery stayed in business because a generous benefactor contributed money to pay for expenses not covered by income from doughnut sales.

4. Which of the following activities are *benign*?

   ____Boomerang naps in front of a mouse hole.

   ____Rosco uses Boomerang as an errand boy.

   ____ Boomerang eats Rosco's winter supply of Munster cheese.

   ____Rosco regularly teases the watchdog.

   ____Rosco eats the carrot-nose of a snowman.

   Name_____

I HAVE A PENCHANT FOR CREATING CHEESE SCULPTURES.

penchant

(n) a strong taste or liking for something

1. Do you share Rosco's *penchant* (as shown in the cartoons)?

   If not, name one of your *penchants*.

2. Write a different person's name to finish each of these sentences.

   a. _____ has a penchant for chocolate.

   b. It's clear that_____has no penchant for cooking.

   c. _____ has a greater penchant for math than does_____ .

   d. _____ has a penchant for movies.

   e. _____ has little penchant for homework.

   f. _____'s penchant for _____ is exceeded only by his

      (or her) penchant for _____ .

   g. _____has minimal penchant for_____.
      (your name)

3. Mark S if the word is a synonym for *penchant*. Mark A if it is an antonym.

   ___ fondness

   ___ loathing

   ___ relish

   ___ affinity

   ___ proclivity

   ___ aversion

   ___ abhorrence

   ___ attraction

I ALSO HAVE AN EQUALLY COMPELLING PENCHANT FOR EATING THEM!

Name_____

irascible

(adj) easily angered; irritable

1. Portia Mouse explains why she's *irascible*. List at least five other factors or situations that could cause someone to be *irascible*.

2. Draw your own picture or diagram to convey the idea of the word *irascible*.

YOU'D BE IRASIBLE TOO, IF YOU HAD A CRAZY CAT DOGGING YOU!

3. As you read the story, look for words that have meanings similar to or opposite from *irascible*. Circle words that support an *irascible* feeling, and draw a box around words with an opposite meaning or feeling.

The amiable rat, Rosco, invited his good friend to join him on a fun escapade to scrounge for food. But just minutes into the calm outing, a box with half a pepperoni pizza changed everything. Ornery snarls shattered the tranquil evening. The usually-generous friend became a cantankerous cat, hoarding the entire food find for himself. Hunger had turned him livid at the thought of sharing. So the tolerant Rosco turned away from his cranky friend to munch on some scraps of moldy bread.

Name_____

extricate

(v) set or get free from an entanglement
or difficulty

HEY, THIS ISN'T
FUNNY ANY MORE!

1. Rosco needs some help. Make one
or more suggestions about how to
extricate him from the situation in
the cartoon.

2. Write a brief answer for each example.

   a. What have you done to extricate yourself from an embarrassing situation?

   b. Who or what might need to be extricated from a trap?

   c. How would you extricate yourself from a wet suit?

   d. Who or what might wish to be extricated from a spider web?

   e. From where would you extricate gold?

   f. How could someone be extricated from a harmful relationship?

3. Say the word *extricate*
and listen for the word
trick within it. Explain
to a classmate or
friend how *trick* can
help you remember the
meaning of *extricate*.

4. A dentist might *extract* a tooth. This word has a
similar sound and meaning to *extricate*, but is not
quite the same. Find the meaning. Then write a
sentence using both words correctly.

Name_____

acute *(adj)* sharp; severe (but usually lasts a short time)

chronic *(adj)* ever present; lasting a long time

BOOMERANG'S ACUTE LAZINESS IS BECOMING CHRONIC!

1. How does the comic strip convey the idea of *acute* laziness?

2. How does the comic strip convey the idea of *chronic* laziness?

3. Describe some evidence for each of the situations. (How could you tell that it's happening or that it is true? What might you see or hear?)

acute pain

chronically annoying dog

an acute sense of humor

chronic confusion in math class

chronic difficulty finding his way around

an acute sense of fairness

Name_____

Vocabulary Escapades—Learning Adventures Series

furtive

(adj) stealthy; secretive

1. What does the word *furtive* bring to your mind? Write ten or more words or phrases (moods, sounds, actions, ideas, feelings, names, places, titles, events, etc.)

2. Imagine what Boomerang has done (or is about to do) that results in this *furtive* look. Briefly describe your idea with a sentence or phrase.

3. Which sentences use *furtive* or a form of it correctly? (Circle the letters.)

   a. He had the furtive look of someone with something to hide.

   b. Her furtive glances at her watch gave me the idea that she wanted to leave.

   c. We suspected that his fortune had been obtained furtively.

   d. The bully's threats were furtive because no one was scared.

   e. Wasn't that furtive of the thief to steal the statue in broad daylight?

4. If Boomerang is involved in a *furtive* scheme to raid the pantry, which of these words should probably not be used to describe his plan? (Circle the words.)

SNEAKY   forthright   HIDDEN   CLANDESTINE   aboveboard

brazen   private   underhanded   covert   MASKED

SURREPTITIOUS   undercover   public   SHIFTY   wily

Name_____

   40

inevitable

(adj) unavoidable; certain

1. What does Rosco Rat guess is *inevitable?*

2. Why do you think he sees this as *inevitable?*

3. Which sentences contain a word or phrase that has a meaning similar to *inevitable?* (Circle the letters.)

    a. The peanut brittle was so stale that it was inedible.

    b. It was inconceivable that Portia Mouse would accept Boomerang's gift.

    c. Wasn't it a foregone conclusion that Boomerang's heart would get broken?

    d. Rosco gave good advice, but Boomerang was fated to ignore it..

4. Describe what you think is an *inevitable* outcome for each of these.

The math teacher announces a surprise pop quiz to the class.

Two nine-month-old babies are put into one playpen with one toy.

A cat sees a mouse.

Five rats are left alone in a room with a cream-puff sculpture.

Name_____

adjudicate

(v) to decide upon as a judge

1. What do you think about the judge's *adjudication?*

2. *Adjudicate* three or more of these cases below. Fill in the blanks to finish the sentences or lines.

CASE 1

Neighbors in Maxie's street have sued her for property damage. The charge is that Maxie's dog Max has been allowed to run free, destroying gardens, lawns, and fences in the neighborhood. Max was impounded with shreds of Mr. Gross's fence in his teeth. Samples of Ms. Green's new grass were scraped from Max's tongue, and petals from Mrs. Pinkie's prize roses were on his paws. Dirt from another garden was found under his nails. Maxie claims the group of neighbors framed her dog. The judge decides _____

CASE 2

Charlie Citrus is charged with pillaging a lemonade stand. The prosecutor shows evidence that he was near the scene of the crime. Lemon rinds in his shoes, sticky palms, and lemon seeds in his ears are cited as evidence. Charlie claims he was making lemonade at home when he had to run to the nearby lemon stand for more lemons. He was there, but he didn't steal anything, he insists. Is there enough evidence to convict him? His lawyer says, "No." The judge rules _____

CASE 3

The adjudication was announced before three

On custody of a young chimpanzee

The judgment was fast

The lawyers were aghast

For the judge _____

CASE 4

A case came before Judge Jay Jude:

A lawsuit against guys who were rude.

Said the judge,

"_____

_____,"

As he looked at the ones who were sued.

Name_____

42

collusion

(v) secret cooperation for deceit

1. These two characters certainly look as if they are in *collusion*. What might they be planning?

BUZZZ BUZZZ

complicit

(adj) participating in guilt

2. J.J. planned a hoax. He asked Desi, Zach, Roxy, Amelia, Darla, Boe, Ceci, and Lana to help. Ceci and Boe declined. The rest snuck into neighbors' gardens at night and pulled up carrots, onions, and other vegetables. The next night Lou joined the group. At midnight, they hung the vegetables on doorknobs, rang the doorbells, and ran away.

Besides J.J., how many people were *complicit* in this trick?____

3. Which statements are conclusions that can logically be drawn from the information on the newspaper? (Circle the letters.)

a. Some cats may be complicit in a crime for helping to steal tuna.

b. Cats reported rats as suspects in a robbery.

c. Police have arrested cats and rats for colluding to break into the factory.

d. Rats are definitely complicit in the disappearance of the tuna.

e. There is evidence that at least one cat and one rat were present at the scene of the break-in.

f. Cats planned the heist.

g. Some police officers are suspected of colluding with the thieves.

Tuesday, May 10

Morning Gazette

Fish Factory Break-In

Fresh Fish Daily

Tons of Tuna Taken

Police Suspect Rat-Cat Collusion

Name_____

THE TALE OF THE
ROYAL WEDDING
OF
PRINCE ERRONEOUS,
THE KINGDOM'S MOST
ILLEGIBLE
BACHELOR

malapropism

(n) a humorous wrong use of a word (usually in place of another word that sounds similiar)

1. Some *malapropisms* are written or spoken on purpose; others are accidental. The story has many accidental *malapropisms*. Circle each one. Above it, write the word that should have been used instead.

The wedding of Prince Erroneous was surrounded with abdominal happenings. Some say the passing of Haley's Comma caused it. Others claim it was a mistake to have planned the wedding on the site where a giant thesaurus had salted twenty cavemen centuries earlier. Afterwards, many thought an evil cruise had been cast upon the prince and his bride.

The village psalm reader looked into her crystal ball and used her extra-century perception to predict trouble. The king devised the prince to make an altercation in the time and place, but the wedding was planned. So the prince went ahead with his plans for acrimony. He just took it for granite that everything would turn out fine, telling his advisors that the dangers were a pigment of their imaginations.

As the wedding wows began, an explosion rocked the castle, and all the guests had to be quickly evaporated. Flames that spread like wildflowers incarcerated the decorations, the gifts, and even the cake.

What a disaster! Can you phantom how terrible the prince must have felt?

2. The word part *mal* means "wrong" or "bad." Notice how each meaning below contains the idea of "wrong" or "bad." Then match the words on the scroll to their meanings.

   a. clumsy
   b. feeling of depression or queasiness
   c. foul-smelling
   d. showing or causing gloom
   e. poorly adapted to one's environment
   f. habitually dissatisfied
   g. misconduct by a public official
   h. ill will
   i. to speak ill of
   j. a curse
   k. sinister
   l. ailment

   ___malevolent
   ___maladroit
   ___malice
   ___malfeasance
   ___malodorous
   ___malady
   ___maladjusted
   ___malediction
   ___dismal
   ___malcontent
   ___malaise
   ___malign

Name_____

44

sullen

(adj) gloomily silent; dismal

1. What could be the cause of Rosco's *sullen* demeanor?

2. Write a few words or phrases that would describe *sullen* weather.

3. Write a few words or phrases that would describe a *sullen* place.

4. Think of *sullen* as it would describe a person. Fill in the diagram above. The instructions below for A, B, and C tell what to write in each section.

A things or situations that might cause someone to feel or act sullen

B words or phrases that have a meaning similiar to sullen

C word or phrases that have a meaning opposite of sullen

Name_____

restrain

(v) limit or keep under control

1. You probably can't restrain the thunder or the rain, or time, or a runaway train.

   Name at least five other things you cannot restrain.

2. Give an idea for each of these. Tell how someone might *restrain . . .*

   a rat from eating junk food.

   from being rude.

   a temper.

   from talking on a cell phone while driving.

   a pet dog from jumping on people.

   their intake of soda pop.

   from falling asleep in class.

3. A *restraining order* is a legal document obtained from a court. Its purpose is to keep someone from doing something. Name one reason why you think someone might get a *restraining order* against another person.

I NEED A RESTRAINING ORDER!

4. Why might Portia want a *restraining* order?

Name_____

euphony

(n) pleasantly melodic sound

1. Get together with friends or classmates right now and create something that is *euphonious*. What did you do?

cacophony

(n) harsh and unpleasant sound

2. Get together with friends or classmates right now and create something that is *cacophonous*. What did you do?

WHAT A RACKET!
ONE BIRD'S EUPHONY IS ANOTHER RAT'S CACOPHONY!

3. How might someone respond to *cacophony*? Describe one or more behaviors.

4. Rosco Rat seems upset by the bird's singing. Give a reason why the singing might be *cacophonous* to Rosco right now.

   Describe a time when the bird's singing might seem *euphonious*.

5. Decide if the situations on the table are more likely to offer *cacophony* or *euphony*. Put an X in the column of your choice.

	EUPHONY	CACOPHONY
full school bus		
jet runway		
rock concert		
preschool playground		
construction site		
chicken yard		
symphony performance		
ocean side in stormy weather		

Name_____

augment

(v) make bigger; increase or add to

MY WHISKERS ARE ALREADY PERFECT, BUT ROSCO MIGHT BE INTERESTED!

WHISKER AUGMENTATION
Quick, Painless, Affordable
12345 E. Stretch Ave.
Free Consultations, No Obligation

1. How might whiskers be *augmented*?

3. Draw an object of your choice. Then, draw that same object *augmented*.

2. Which of the following would you NOT like to *augment*? (Circle all that apply.)

YOUR GRADE POINT AVERAGE

YOUR BANK ACCOUNT

YOUR TEMPERATURE

YOUR BRAINPOWER

YOUR TROUBLES

THE SCHOOL DAY

LENGTH OF SUMMER

YOUR NUMBER OF FRIENDS

YOUR NOSE

YOUR EYELASHES

HOMEWORK

WEEKENDS

4. Name one thing you would do or choose or need . . .

a. to augment your wardrobe.

b. to augment a meal of pizza and French fries.

c. to augment your knowledge about Black Holes.

d. to augment your physical fitness.

Name_____

48

prominent

(adj) noticeable; distinguished; standing out

1. From clues in the cartoon, what can you guess is *prominent* about Rosco Rat (besides his ego)?

2. Invent a name for a *prominent* person. Make sure the name gives a clear idea that the person is indeed distinguished.

3. Circle any words in these examples that could be replaced with the word *prominent* without changing the meaning.

   a. Gray is the most evident color in Rosco's fur.

   b. Jeff's comic book collection was placed in the most obvious spot in his room.

   c. She used a lot of makeup to cover the conspicuous scar.

   d. The beak on that pelican is his most protrusive feature.

   e. Rosco's cleverness is his most prestigious attribute.

   f. My, what jutting teeth that wolf has!

4. Draw something *prominent* that has not been mentioned on this page.

5. FIND OUT WHAT A PROMONTORY IS. WOULD YOU SAY A PROMONTORY IS PROMINENT?

Name_____

deduction

(n) process of reaching a conclusion by reasoning from general principles; the conclusion that is reached by this process

(n) act of subtracting; the amount that is or may be subtracted

1. What could be the background experience or fact that led Rosco to his *deduction?*

2. There are six houses on the block with a total of seven pet cats. One house has no pets. The Green family lives between the Yoders and the Smiths. The Smiths have no pets. Tommy Green concludes that the Yoders have two cats. Is his *deduction* reasonable?

3. From the information given in #2 above, what can you *deduce* about the number of cats in the Green house?

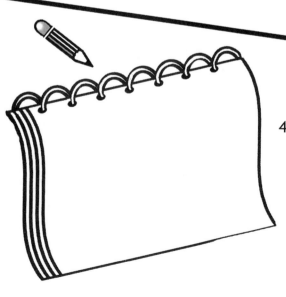

4. A family calculating U.S. income tax for 2010 could *deduct* from its total income $3650 for each child and $11,400 for the couple. Mr. and Mrs. Yoder have three small children. Before the *deductions*, their income was at $52,000.

Deduct the *deductions* to find the income on which they were taxed.

Name_____

50

exuberant

(adj) joyfully unrestrained

I'M EXUBERANT!

EXHILARATED! ECSTATIC! EXASPERATED!

JOYFUL! **PROUD!** LETHARGIC! BLUE!

ELATED! OVERJOYED! **RESTRAINED!**

EXCAVATED! DELIGHTED!

1. Which words in Rosco's thought bubble do not fit with his *exuberance*? (Cross them out.)

2. Name five situations or events that would cause you to be *exuberant*.

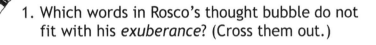

3. Draw or design the word *exuberant* in a way that shows what it means.

4. Imagine a cartoon character who is chronically *exuberant*. What would be a good name for this character?

_____

Name_____

ambivalence

(n) the state of having opposing or
conflicting feelings at the same time

MY DEVOTION
TO PORTIA IS
NEVER
AMBIVALENT.

BUT I'M VERY
CONFLICTED ABOUT THE
NEED FOR LIMA BEANS
IN MY DIET.

1. Conduct a quick survey of students in your class
or any other group of people that is near you at
this time. Take a count of how many of these
people have *ambivalent* feelings about each
of the following.

    Number of people surveyed:____

    ___getting a job   ___romance

    ___research papers   ___dancing

    ___riding roller coasters   ___spicy foods

    ___school dress codes   ___homework

    ___singing in public   ___dress codes

    ___hip-hop music   ___video games

2. How does the comic strip
reflect *ambivalence*?

3. Identify something about which you feel little or no *ambivalence*.

4. Circle the word that best completes each analogy.

   a. _____ : ambivalent :: benign : kindly

   indecisive   **certainty**   **confident**   **mistake**

   b. important : importance :: _____ : ambivalence

   ambiance   **clashing**   **ambivalent**   **fear**

   c. ambivalence : _____ :: eschew: embrace

   wavering   **certainty**   **decision**   **impatience**

Name_____

52

inordinate

(adj) unusual; excessive

1. What portion of Boomerang's order would you say is *inordinate*?

2. Finish at least five of the sentences.

There is an inordinate amount of poverty in_____ .

_____ spends an inordinate amount of time_____ .

In my school or community, I notice an inordinate waste of _____ .

You would find an inordinate number of teenagers at (or in)_____ .

_____owns an inordinate supply of_____ .

_____spends an inordinate amount of money on_____ .

There are an inordinate number of_____in my room.

3. Circle words that are not similar in meaning to *inordinate*.

moderate
extravagant
outrageous
superfluous
reasonable
unnecessary
inhibited
unrestrained
sensible
superabundant

4. Write a sentence with an *inordinate* number of words to express this idea:

The bakery makes great doughnuts.

Name_____

I'LL ELICIT THE LOCATION OF THE ILLICIT GOODS.

elicit

(v) bring out; draw forth

illicit

(adj) unlawful

1. Private Investigator Rosco has been hired to investigate the theft of a shipment of mouse traps. What might be his motivation for taking this case?

2. From whom might the detective *elicit* information about the location of the mouse traps?

3. Briefly answer the questions.

   • What could be elicited from a jury at a trial? _____

   • What illicit activity might happen at a mall? _____

   • Who might be able to elicit truth from a liar? _____

   • What might you elicit from a grandmother? _____

   • Is sneezing an illicit behavior? _____

4. Which sentences below use both *illicit* and *elicit* (or forms of them) correctly?

   a. The detective interviewed several witnesses, trying to elicit clues about the illicit activities taking place near the school property.

   b. Maxie Moolah was caught elicitly illiciting money from an ATM machine.

   c. If you can't illicit the truth from your friend, she might bamboozle you into elicit ventures.

   d. It's easy to remember *illicit*, because it means illegal. But it's harder to elicit from my brain a way to remember the meaning of *elicit*.

Name_____

vacillate

(v) fluctuate; be indecisive

MENU

Lasagna..............$3.50 per serving
Spaghetti.............$2.99 per serving
3 Tacos...............$3.25
Sandwiches.........$3.75 each
Pastrami   Tuna Fish   Swiss Cheese
Burrito.................$2.75
Cheese Pizza.......$2.50 per slice
Cheese Soufflé.....$4.50

1. Rosco Rat can't make up his mind! Why do you think he is *vacillating* about this?

2. Name three things about which you are likely to *vacillate*.

3. Write a brief answer for each question. What could cause *vacillation* . . .

   AT AN AMUSEMENT PARK?

   IN A SCIENCE LAB?

   AT A SCHOOL DANCE?

   ON A HIKE?

   DURING A MATH TEST?

   AT A MOVIE THEATER?

I'LL HAVE THE SWISS CHEESE SANDWICH . . .

WAIT! I'LL TAKE LASAGNA . . .

NO, I WANT THE PIZZA . . .

I STILL WANT THE PIZZA . . .

OR, MAYBE, A CHEESE SOUFFLÉ . . .

4. Suppose Rosco was offered two free tickets to a favorite rock concert at the same time as his friend Boomerang's birthday party? What might be the effect of his *vacillation*?

Name_____

faux

(adj) false; fake

1. What is *faux* about the situation in the cartoon?

2. How many *faux* things are mentioned in the poem?

> HE GAVE HER ROSES.
> THEY WERE PLASTIC—
> NOT THE KIND THAT GROW.
>
> HE MADE HER PROMISES.
> THEY WERE BROKEN.
> "YES, DEAR," TURNED INTO "NO."
>
> HE BRAGGED OF RICHES,
> BUT THERE WERE DEBTS.
> THERE WASN'T ANY DOUGH.
>
> HE BROUGHT A DIAMOND—
> AND IT WAS FAKE.
> THE GEM WAS JUST FOR SHOW.
>
> AS IT TURNED OUT,
> THE GIFTS, ROMANCE,
> AND THE BOY HIMSELF—WERE FAUX.

3. Sometimes *faux* is acceptable. Sometimes it is not. Which of these could be okay, and which would you reject for yourself or in someone else? Write **Y** (yes) or **N** (no) for each one.

I can put up with faux . . .

__promises	__artwork
__teeth	__tickets to a ballgame
__hair color	__tarantulas
__jewelry	__tans
__friendships	__diplomas
__names	__designer jeans
__illnesses	__ fingernails
__boyfriend	__ girlfriend
__sympathy	__driver's license (ID)

Name_____

genius

(n) a person with mental superiority
(adj) exceptionally brilliant

prodigy

(n) extraordinary accomplishment, person,
or event; a child with great talent or skills

> I WAS ONCE A PRODIGY IN SNOOPING, SNIFFING, AND SNATCHING.

> NOW THAT I'M OLDER, I'M CONSIDERED A GENIUS AT RODENT SURVIVAL.

1. Given the information that you can find in the cartoon, is Rosco's claim valid?

_____

Explain your answer.

2. The word *genius* can also be used as an adjective, meaning exceptionally brilliant. Name an idea or invention that you believe is *genius*.

3. For each example, decide whether (or not) the person is probably a *genius* or a *prodigy* or both. Place an X in the space that shows your decision (yes, no, or NEI for "There is not enough information to tell.")

Description	GENIUS?			PRODIGY?		
	Yes	No	NEI	Yes	No	NEI
At age six, Zerah Colburn could multiply six-digit numbers in his head.						
Ruth Lawrence entered Oxford University as a math student at age 11.						
Akrit Jaswal, India's youngest university student and medical doctor, was performing surgeries at age seven.						
At age 12, Lexi Thompson was the youngest golfer to qualify for the U. S. Women's Open tournament. In 2010, at age 15, she became the youngest female golfer to turn professional.						

Name_____

57

gesture

(n) use of motions (usually limbs or body) to express ideas, emotions, or attitudes

gesticulate

(v) make gestures, especially when speaking

1. Watch as Rosco and his friends *gesticulate*, and try to interpret their *gestures*. In each case, fill in the bubble to show what he or she is thinking.

2. Briefly give some important advice to another person or group (right now, if you can). *Gesticulate* in a way that helps to communicate your message.

   Describe one or more of the *gestures* you used.

3. Not all *gestures* are appropriate in all situations. Some are rude. Some are easily misinterpreted. Some can get you into trouble. Other *gestures* are never a good idea.

   Make a mental list of *gestures* that you know are best if avoided.

Name_____

futile

(adj) unsuccessful; useless

First Prize for the largest cheesecake 1000 pounds

Keep 15 feet away from the exhibit!

ADMIRABLE, BUT FUTILE!

1. What is it that Rosco is calling admirable, but *futile*?

2. What things would probably be the opposite of *futile* for a hungry rat?

3. Finish the sentences with your ideas (not related to the comic strip).

a. It would be futile to try_____.

b. _____was a futile idea.
   (Some event or effort in recent or past history.)

c. Something that seems is futile, but I wish were not, is_____.

d. _____is less futile than _____.

Name_____

innovation

(n) new idea or method

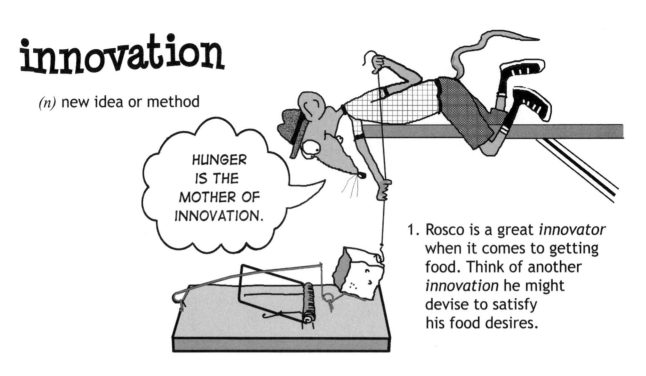

HUNGER IS THE MOTHER OF INNOVATION.

1. Rosco is a great *innovator* when it comes to getting food. Think of another *innovation* he might devise to satisfy his food desires.

2. Name your favorite *innovation* in each category below:

DIGITAL TECHNOLOGY

SIMPLE GADGETS

EDIBLE

MUSICAL

CLOTHING

GAME OR RECREATION

ENTERTAINMENT

MOVEMENT OR TRANSPORTATION

OTHER:

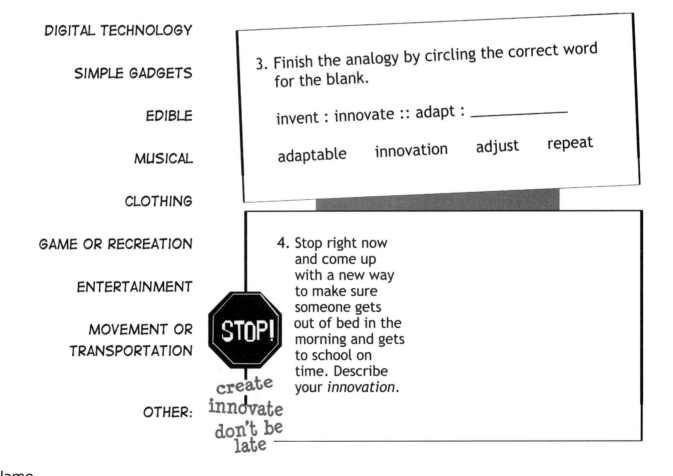

3. Finish the analogy by circling the correct word for the blank.

invent : innovate :: adapt : _____

adaptable   innovation   adjust   repeat

4. Stop right now and come up with a new way to make sure someone gets out of bed in the morning and gets to school on time. Describe your *innovation*.

create innovate don't be late

Name_____

obstruct

(v) block; impede; slow down

1. What might Rosco be trying to *obstruct*? (Suggest two or more ideas.)

2. Give a brief explanation or idea as to how each of the things listed could be *obstructed*.

AN INN**O**VATION

BREATHING

AN INVE**S**TIGATION

JUS**T**ICE

F**R**EEDOM

A VIEW O**U**T A WINDOW

TRAFFI**C**

ENTRY **T**O A BUILDING

DON'T EVEN THINK ABOUT IT!

3. Draw a picture or diagram to show each of these being *obstructed*.

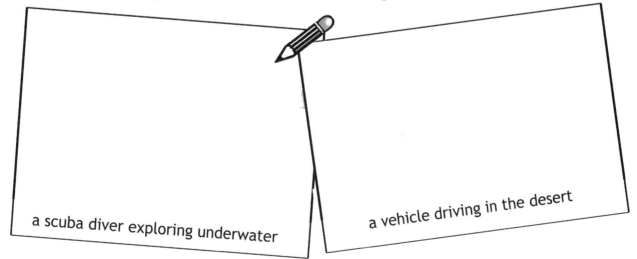

a scuba diver exploring underwater

a vehicle driving in the desert

Name_____

chaos

(n) complete disorder

HERE'S MY ESSAY ABOUT HOW WELL CATS HANDLE CHAOS.

A+

1. Name a place besides Rosco's bedroom that might be the picture of *chaos*.

2. What would *chaos* in a school cafeteria look like?

3. What or who might cause *chaos* on a city street?

4. What is the most *chaotic* place in your life?

CHAOS? WHAT CHAOS?

5. Name three things that could cause *chaos* at an airport.

6. What might be the effects of *chaos* in a mall?

7. How might weather cause *chaos*?

Name_____

62

jeopardize

(v) expose to loss or danger

THANKS, PAL.

WHAT DO I LOOK LIKE — A FLOOR MAT?

1. How might Rosco's actions (shown in the cartoon) *jeopardize* his relationship with Boomerang?

2. Give an idea for each example below. What could *jeopardize* . . .

YOUR HEALTH?

A FRIENDSHIP?

YOUR REPUTATION?

YOUR GRADE IN ENGLISH CLASS?

YOUR SAFETY ON THE HIGHWAY?

YOUR CREDIBILITY?

THE FUTURE OF THE PLANET?

THE SUCCESS OF A PARTY?

YOUR ALLOWANCE?

THE RIGHT TO FREE SPEECH?

3. *Jeopardy* (a noun) means exposure to loss or danger. Draw or describe a leopard in *jeopardy*.

4. *Jeopardy* is also the danger that an accused person is in when on trial for a crime. Laws prohibit a person from being in *double jeopardy*. Make an inference as to what this means.

Name_____

paucity

(n) shortage

THERE WAS A PLETHORA OF TASTY FOOD IN HERE ON MONDAY— BUT A PAUCITY OF PICKINGS TODAY.

WHY IS THAT, I WONDER?

GARBAGE DAY!

plethora

(n) excess

1. Write a sentence to summarize the complaint Rosco has made about the garbage situation. Do not use any of these words: *paucity, plethora, shortage, excess.*

2. Create a poster of a complaint (using the words *paucity* and *plethora*) that you would post in your house, school, or town.

3. Think about the amount of each of these things in your culture or in the world. Is there a *paucity* or *plethora* of it (them)? Show your opinion by marking **PA** for *paucity*, **PL** for *plethora*, or **R** for the right amount.

__food

__clean air

__TV shows

__bugs

__education

__stores

__parks

__police services

__clothes

__love

__anger

__waste

You add three:

_____

_____

_____

Name_____

bane

(n) cause of distress or suffering; poison

I'M ALWAYS HERE FOR YOU, PORTIA.

Boomerang - the bane of Portia's existence

THAT'S THE PROBLEM, NOT THE SOLUTION.

1. What else might Boomerang communicate or do that would add to Portia's distress?

2. Give at least one idea to answer each question. What would be a *bane* for . . .

YOUR EXISTENCE?   SOMEONE TRYING TO SLEEP?

A COMEDIAN?   THE PILOT OF A JET FIGHTER PLANE?

A KID TRYING TO FINISH HIS/HER HOMEWORK?   A CHILDREN'S DOCTOR?

---

3. Look at the words and phrases that are **synonyms** for *bane*. Each time *bane* is used below, cross it out and substitute something from the list.

   a. Oh, king, beware! There's bane in that goblet!

   b. Her little brother is a bane when her boyfriend visits.

   c. "A bane on you!" cried the evil witch, as she turned the prince into a frog.

   d. That nosy neighbor is the bane of Louella's existence.

   e. Her paralyzed tongue was a constant bane as she tried to take part in the gossip.

burden
PLAGUE SCOURGE
curse
torment affliction
BLIGHT
WOE
annoyance nuisance
A THORN IN THE SIDE
A PAIN IN THE NECK
A FLY IN THE OINTMENT

Name_____

obsequious *(adj)* excessively flattering or attentive; sucking up to

1. Usually, someone makes *obsequious* comments or behaves in an *obsequious* manner because she or he is hoping for a particular result. What might be the purpose of Rosco's *obsequious* behavior toward Meatball?

2. The word *sycophant* means "someone who is habitually *obsequious*." Fill in each talk balloon with an example of an *obsequious* comment that a *sycophant* might make in the situation.

to a parent

at a restaurant

to a coach, principal, police officer, or other authority figure

other (You decide.)

3. Many people confuse the word *obsequious* with the word *ubiquitous*. Which sentences use one or both words correctly?

   a. Goodness! Obsequious teacher's pets are ubiquitous in this school!

   b. Julia was so obsequious to all her classmates that it was impossible to tell how she really felt about any of them.

   c. These mosquitoes are obsequious! I can't get rid of them!

   d. I'm not impressed with my boyfriend's ubiquitous behavior. I think it's phony.

Name_____

irony

(n) use of words to express the opposite of what is really meant; incongruity between actual and expected results of an event

Irony has nothing to do with ironing. However, it would be an *irony* to give an iron as a gift to a person (or rat) who has no clothes. It would also be *ironic* if an iron salesman came to your door in a badly wrinkled suit. Briefly explain the *irony* in the comic strip and each story below.

1. The *irony* is _____

_____

An author is anxious to sell her new book, **How to Protect Your Privacy**. She decides to advertise it heavily on her FaceBook page. She hopes that many of her 148 FaceBook friends will decide to purchase a copy.

Martin missed his 7th period physical education class three days in a row last week. He stayed in the library through those classes because he had to finish a paper for English that was due on Friday. The paper was titled: "The Many Benefits of Regular Exercise."

2. The *irony* is _____

_____

_____

3. The *irony* is _____

_____

_____

Name_____

DON'T EVEN TRY TO CHANGE MY MIND!

obstinate

(adj) stubborn in sticking to
an opinion, attitude, or course of action

1. Describe three events or situations that might cause Rosco to be *obstinate*.

2. Circle any word in the poem that has a meaning similar to *obstinate*.

OBSTINATE OLIVE
STUBBORN AS A MULE,
MUST HAVE IT HER WAY,
BREAKS EVERY RULE.

INFLEXIBLE AS STEEL,
NOT COMPLIANT IN A PINCH,
WON'T CHANGE HER MIND,
SHE DOESN'T GIVE AN INCH.

COMPROMISE IS OUT,
RECALCITRANT IS IN.
SHE'S PIGHEADED, INSISTENT
THAT NO ONE ELSE CAN WIN.

OBDURATE OLIVE
HEADSTRONG IN SCHOOL,
IF YOU CALLED HER "DOCILE,"
THEN YOU'D BE A FOOL!

3. When was the last time you were *obstinate*? (Briefly explain the circumstances.)

4. There is a proverb that says this:

A FOOL IS BETTER THAN AN OBSTINATE MAN.

Tell why you agree or disagree with the proverb.

Name_____

loathe
(v) hate

loath
(adj) very reluctant

loathing
(n) extreme disgust

loathsome
(adj) repulsive

I LOATHE ANYTHING THAT MAKES ME SWEAT!

1. Choose the correct word (from the four above) to compete each sentence.

   a. Rosco finds it _____to be outwitted by a dog.

   b. He seems to_____ hard work of any kind.

   c. He is particularly _____to find a regular job.

   d. The idea of paying for his ill-gotten gains is extremely

   _____to him.

   e. Rosco looks at his pursuer with fear and _____.

2. Draw or name something else a rat might *loathe*.

3. Draw or name something you would be *loath* to eat.

4. Name a behavior that an adult you know regards with *loathing*.

5. Draw or describe something that is *loathsome* to you.

Name_____

piracy *(n)* robbery on the high seas   *(n)* use of someone else's invention or property without permission

1. The DENOTATION of a word is its definition. This page gives two denotations for *piracy*. What kind of things might be stolen through the kind of *piracy* suggested by the outfits in the cartoon?

ARE YE READY FOR A SPOT OF PIRACY, MATEY?

AYE, AYE, CAP'N!

2. Name something that might be stolen through the kind of *piracy* described in the other denotation.

3. The CONNOTATION of a word is much broader than its denotation. Connotation is all the additional meanings, ideas, impressions, or suggestions that are associated with the word. Think about the connotation of one or both meanings of *piracy*. Write words and phrases to describe all the images that come to your mind (things, settings, situations, people, places, events, sights, emotions, etc).

Name_____

bona fide

(adj) genuine; the real thing; done in good faith

1. How could someone tell for sure that Ratman is a *bona fide* superhero?

2. List some characteristics of a *bona fide* friend.

3. The word *bona fide* comes from a Latin phrase meaning "in good faith," or "without fraud or deceit." Which of the following assurances is most likely to be *bona fide*?

   a. The owner of a car dealership takes in his cousin's ex-girlfriend's 1999 Ford Thunderbird. He sells it to you with the assurance that it is in tip-top shape.

   b. J.J. has not done well in math all semester. His parents have received several calls from the teacher about the absence of completed homework. Today, J.J. brought home a report card with an A in math (a slightly smudged A). He assured his parents that he had worked hard and brought his grade up.

   c. Willy received a large check as an inheritance from rich Uncle William. The bank and the law firm assure him that the check is valid.

4. Write three words or phrases that could be used to describe something that is NOT *bona fide*.

Name_____

collaborate

(v) work jointly with others

1. Name three or more situations in which you believe it is absolutely necessary for people to *collaborate*.

2. A group of pizza chefs will *collaborate* to build a giant, record-breaking pizza. What do you think should or might happen first?

3. What will probably be the results of the *collaboration* shown in the cartoon?

Our Musical Collaboration

4. Stop and *collaborate* (with some classmates or friends) to write one verse of song lyrics. Use *collaborate* or some form of it. Here are some other words that might be helpful.

COOPERATE ELABORATE CALCULATE
EVAPORATE PERPETRATE OPERATE
EXCAVATE INVESTIGATE IMITATE
DELEGATE NEGOTIATE DUPLICATE
SEPARATE TOLERATE HESITATE

Name_____

72

novel

(adj) new or strange

1. Read the two thought bubbles.
Suggest a *novel* way to write a new
sign for the store's cheese platter.

novice

(n) someone untrained or
inexperienced at a task or skill

2. Invent a *novel* way to sharpen
a pencil. Describe it.

3. Finish the sentences.

When it comes to_____, I am a novice.

_____is a novice at _____.
(someone else's name)

4. A *novel* is also a long fictional
story. Imagine yourself coming
up with a *novel* idea for a *novel*
about a *novice*.

Tell something about your main
character and about what the
main conflict or problem of the
novel would be.

Name_____

induce

(v) persuade; bring about

1. How does the word *induce* relate to the comic strip? (What is *induced*? And what is responsible for the *inducing*?)

2. Stop right now and *induce* someone to do one or more of these:

- dance with you

- tell you a joke

- draw a picture of a cartoon character

- growl like a hungry cat on a diet

- sing "Row, Row, Row Your Boat"

- share an embarrassing memory

3. Suggest an idea about what might *induce* each of these:

SLEEP

SOMEONE TO BUY A RAFFLE TICKET

A TSUNAMI

A HEADACHE

YOU TO DONATE MONEY

A RIOT

SOMEONE TO BUY A NEW CELL PHONE

Name_____

74

dire

(adj) extreme; nearly hopeless; causing fear or dread

1. What do you think the *dire* circumstances are in the cartoon?

What would be a *dire* remedy?

4. In your opinion, which of these are NOT examples of *dire* problems?

____ a broken arm
____ a tornado approaching
____ a teenager that constantly drives recklessly
____ a broken fingernail
____ a missed piano lesson
____ a group of kids sharing illegal drugs
____ a missed homework assignment
____ a family without food
____ a disappearing polar bear population

2. What kind of news might be *dire*?

5. Where have you seen or been in a *dire* situation? Draw or describe it.

3. When might a fire cause a *dire* emergency?

Name_____

75

philanthropy

(n) a desire to improve the well-being of humans; an active effort toward this improvement (such as through donations of money, property, or work); a particular organization that promotes human welfare

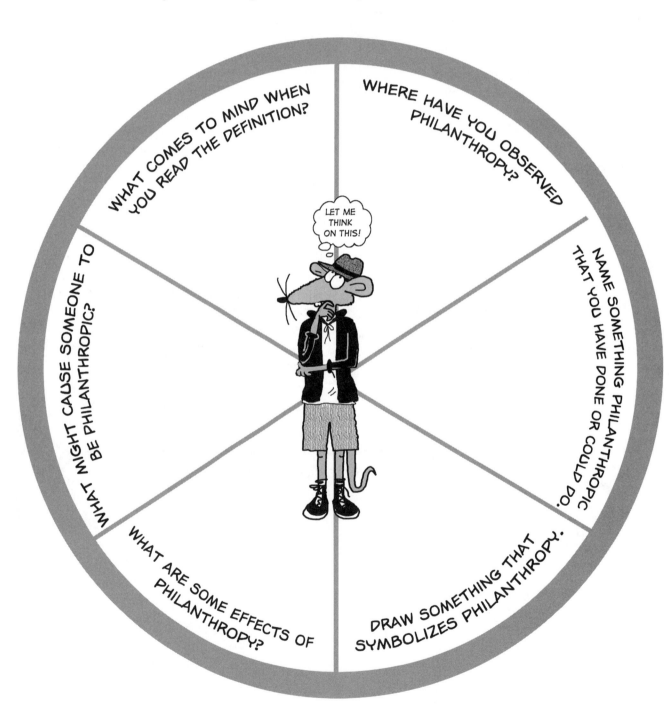

WHAT COMES TO MIND WHEN YOU READ THE DEFINITION?

WHERE HAVE YOU OBSERVED PHILANTHROPY?

NAME SOMETHING PHILANTHROPIC THAT YOU HAVE DONE OR COULD DO.

DRAW SOMETHING THAT SYMBOLIZES PHILANTHROPY.

WHAT ARE SOME EFFECTS OF PHILANTHROPY?

WHAT MIGHT CAUSE SOMEONE TO BE PHILANTHROPIC?

LET ME THINK ON THIS!

Name_____

TRY OUR NEW SEAWEED AND FRIED WORM SANDWICH. IT'S A DELICACY THAT'S SURE TO BE THE LATEST TASTE SENSATION.

I FEEL NAUSEA COMING ON!

nauseous

(adj) causing disgust or a sick feeling in the stomach

1. It is said that rats will eat anything. If this sandwich **appealed** to Rosco, what word might he use instead of *nauseous*?

2. List what is *nauseous* to you for each category.

FOOD _____

_____

BEHAVIOR _____

_____

MUSIC _____

_____

ACTIVITY _____

_____

3. How is the poem connected to the word *nauseous*?

I'd never eat an oyster because
The taste I could not stand.
I'd rather swallow goldfish live
Or chew a live rock band.

I'd eat my I-Pod, eat the tunes,
Chew on earphones every day.
But put an oyster on my tongue?
Not! Never! No way!

You could torture me with scorpions,
Hang pythons from my walls,
Fill my bathtub with piranhas,
Push me over Niagara Falls.

You could swear to light my underwear,
Dunk me in boiling water to my hips.
No matter what you threaten
No oyster will ever touch my lips.

Joel Fischer, Gr 8

4. Circle the phrase that most effectively shows that the writer feels *nauseous* about his subject.

Name_____

pugilist

(n) a boxer

Bruiser Boomerang suffered a sharp jab to the solar plexus and fell against the ropes with a boom.

1. The word *pugilist* shares a root (*pug*) with several other words. Find the meanings of the words *pugnacious, impugn,* and *repugnant.* Use at least two of them in a sentence about the *pugilist* in the cartoon.

2. Finish the analogies.

   a. pugilism : boxing :: pilfering : _____
       reading   injury   stealing   farming

   b. _____: pugilist :: stethoscope : physician
       headache   heal   fight   gloves

   c. delightful : repugnant :: _____ : vulgar
       elegant   fight   tacky   tasteless

4. Think of a good name for a *pugilist.*

3. Give a brief answer to each question.

   Would you get into an altercation with a pugilist?

   Does your school encourage pugilism on school grounds?

   What might be repugnant to a pugilist?

   What might someone say to impugn a pugilist?

   Would it be a good idea to impugn a pugnacious neighbor?

   Name_____

slander

(v) to say false and damaging things about someone

(n) false and damaging things spoken about someone

libel

(v) to publish damaging misinformation about someone

(n) damaging misinformation published about someone

1. Which of the places or items shown in the cartoon could be sources of *slander*?

2. Which of the places or items shown in the cartoon could be sources of *libel*?

3. The word *liable* sounds like *libel*. One of its meanings is "likely." What group(s) of people are most *liable* to be *libeled*?

4. What might someone do to *slander* a magician?

5. Read the headline and the statement. Label each one as possible *slander* or *libel*.

ROSCO RAT STOLE THE CROWN JEWELS AND USED THEM AS FISH TANK DECORATIONS!

_____

_____

Name_____

inane

(adj) silly or stupid

1. What is *inane* about this cartoon?

YOUR HONOR, MY INANE CLIENT WISHES TO PLEAD INANITY!

2. Read the definition. What does this bring to your mind? Watch the clock or set a timer for one minute. In that amount of time, write all the things that come to your mind that have any connection to the word *inane*.

3. Finish each line to name or describe something *inane*.

_____ lost in Spain

_____ caught in the rain

_____ on a train

_____ with a giant brain

_____ driving a crane

_____ down the drain

_____ using a cane

_____

_____

(On the last two lines, write anything that will rhyme with inane.)

Name_____

ROSCO FLAUNTS HIS NEW SKATEBOARD . . .

ABSOLUTELY **NO** SKATEBOARDS IN THE GYM

flaunt
(v) show off

flout
(v) disregard; treat with scorn

. . . WHILE FLOUTING THE RULES OF THE GYM.

1. What else (besides things mentioned in the captions) does Rosco Rat *flaunt* or *flout* in the cartoon?

4. What rule is most frequently *flouted* in your school or home?

2. Name a skill or possession that you sometimes *flaunt* or that you would *flaunt* if you had it.

3. For each of these, decide if you think someone would be more likely to *flaunt* it or *flout* it . . .

   A BROKEN LEG?

   A YELLOW TRAFFIC LIGHT?

   A "NO TRESPASSING" SIGN?

   A TROPHY?

   AN A+ ON A TEST?

5. Finish the poems by filling in the missing lines.

WE'RE ALL DAUNTED BY SAM'S WEALTH AND POWER. HE SEEMS TO FLAUNT IT

_____

The library sign reads "Quiet at all times." Lulu flouts the rule

_____

Name_____

metaphor

(n) a comparison of two unlike things; use of words to suggest a likeness between two things that are different

MY PAL BOOMERANG IS CREAM CHEESE ON THE CRACKER OF LIFE.

1. Rosco uses a *metaphor* to make a comment about his friend. Think about your friends. Write your own *metaphor* about friends or friendship.

2. For each of the *metaphors* below, tell what things are being compared.

   a. Her smile is chocolate syrup for my soul.

   b. That cluttered closet is a garbage dump.

   c. The battle with Algebra is over; the treaty is signed. I passed.

3. A *simile* is a specific kind of *metaphor* that compares things using the words *like* or *as*. These are simpler *metaphors* to create. Finish the following *metaphors* without making them into *similes*. Avoid using the words *like* and *as*. Remember to compare two things that would not ordinarily be seen as similar.

   The science test was_____

   _____is crashing thunder and dark clouds.

   Their romance has been_____

4. Finish this metaphor.

   A good book is

Name_____

prohibit

(v) prevent by some authority

1. From what else could Rosco Rat be *prohibited*?

2. Survey as many people as you can in the next five minutes. Ask which of these things they think should be *prohibited* in schools. On the line in front of each one, write the number of people who responded, "Yes."

_____ MUSIC-PLAYING DEVICES   _____ HOMEWORK   _____ BARE FEET

_____ T-SHIRTS WITH SLOGANS   _____ SHORTS   _____ GUM

_____ WINDOWLESS ROOMS   _____ STRICT TEACHERS   _____ TATTOOS

_____ PIERCINGS   _____ JEANS   _____ CELL PHONES

3. Write or draw a message on each sign to *prohibit* something in the place described.

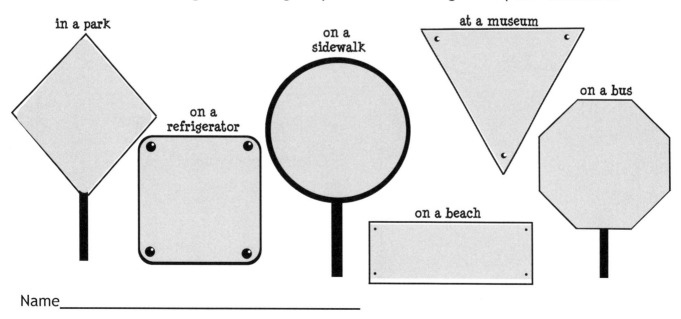

Name_____

aghast

(adj) filled with sudden shock, amazement, fright, or horror

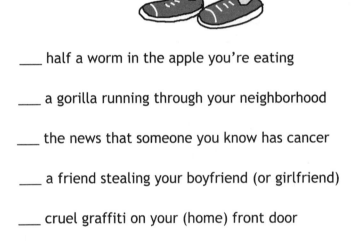

1. What might Boomerang be seeing that has caused him to be *aghast*?

2. Think about how *aghast* you would become at witnessing or experiencing each situation below. Number them in order from 1 to 10, with #1 being "most *aghast*."

___ a $500 cell phone bill

___ a 100% on your vocabulary test

___ your town struck by a tornado

___ someone copying your test answers

___ an amusement park ride stuck with riders upside down

___ half a worm in the apple you're eating

___ a gorilla running through your neighborhood

___ the news that someone you know has cancer

___ a friend stealing your boyfriend (or girlfriend)

___ cruel graffiti on your (home) front door

3. Draw an *aghast* ghost.

4. Finish the limerick.

> The distinguished man was aghast
>
> _____
>
> So without any fuss,
>
> He hopped on a bus
>
> And got of the town really fast!

Name_____

84

postpone

(v) put off until a later time

1. In the cartoon, what is being *postponed*? What tactic is used to cause the *postponement*?

2. Who might *postpone* a ball game?

3. Why might you *postpone* a phone call?

4. Consider each of the following situations. Write each one on the poster where you think it belongs. If a situation belongs on neither one, do not write it at all. Add things of your choice to either poster.

NEVER POSTPONE

ALWAYS POSTPONE

YOUR OWN BIRTHDAY PARTY
RAISE IN YOUR ALLOWANCE
LION-TAMING LESSON
CLEANING YOUR ROOM
SAYING "THANK YOU"
SCHOOL DANCES
PAYING TAXES
VISIT TO THE DENTIST
RABIES SHOT
MAKING AN APOLOGY
BLIND DATE
HOMEWORK
PAYING BILLS
GETTING A JOB
VACATION

Name_____

meander *(v)* follow a twisting route; wander slowly and aimlessly

I HATE PILFERERS.

1. Draw a *meandering* path across this page for Meatball to trail the Cat Burglar. (It's okay if the path passes through the text on the page.)

At different points, draw each of the items below *meandering* across the path.

AN EMPTY CHOCOLATE MILK CARTON

A HALF-EATEN PIZZA

A CAN OF TUNA FISH

A BAG OF KITTY KIBBLE

2. Write a short answer for each of these.

Who or what might meander over a picnic blanket?

What animal travels in a meandering path?

Who or what might meander across a desert?

Where might a river meander?

What would you NOT like to find meandering across your pillow?

Under what conditions might your mind meander?

3.
If it is possible for you to do so, get up and *meander* around the room, house, school, or building. Briefly describe where you walked.

Name_____

amend *(v)* improve; alter or rephrase

1. Rosco Rat decides to write a letter of apology to Boomerang Cat for a careless accident. He hopes he can *amend* the rift in their friendship. Do you think his letter will work? _____

   How would you *amend* the letter to make it better?

2. Name a real-life situation that you think needs to be *amended*.

3. *Amend* each of these sentences to make the meaning clearer.

   a. The blue cat's dish was loaded with food.

   b. Meatball and Boomerang had Rosco for lunch.

   c. Rosco Rat dreams of a cheeseburger snoozing on the couch.

Dear Boomerang,

I'm sorry you are mad at me.

I didn't mean to sit on your ukulele.

I know your grandpa gave it to you, but you shouldn't have left it on the sofa.

I was carrying a full plate of macaroni and cheese and couldn't see where I was going. You should take better care of your things.

your friend,
Rosco Rat

4. The word *amends* can be a noun. It means "a compensation or fix for something that was wrong." People (or rats) can make *amends* for mistakes.

   Rosco frequently pilfers cheese from his neighbors' kitchens. How can he make *amends* for this? (Give two ideas.)

5. Stand up and try to *amend* your posture. Draw a diagram or write a description to tell what you did.

Name_____

literacy *(n)* ability to read and write

1. For each letter of the word, describe something you could **READ** that would demonstrate your *literacy*.

grocery **L**ist
L
I
T
E
R
A
C
Y

2. For each letter of the word, describe something you could **WRITE** that would demonstrate your *literacy*.

P
I
Z
Z
A

L I T E R A C Y

R
E
C
I
P
E
S

3. List some benefits of being *literate*.

4. What books are the cartoon characters reading? Write the title of a book you think each of them is reading.

ROSCO RAT_____

BOOMERANG CAT_____

PORTIA MOUSE_____

MEATBALL BULLDOG_____

Name_____

PORTIA MOUSE IS THE MOST ACRID, ACERBIC, ACRIMONIOUS, PINT-SIZED MOUSE I KNOW!

BUZZ OFF, BEETLE-BREATH!

acrimony
(n) harshness of language or feeling

acrid
(adj) sharp and biting

acerbic
(n) sour and biting in temper, mood, or tone

exacerbate
(v) increase the bitterness or severity of something

1. What clues in the cartoon might lead you to believe that Rosco feels *acrimonious* toward Portia?

2. Describe a situation that you believe could cause *acrimony* between two people.

3. If some *acerbic* words are spoken to Boomerang Cat by Portia, which of these might he hear?
   (Circle all that apply.)

   a compliment   some criticism

   a condemnation   scolding

   congratulations   a commendation

4. Rosco gets a whiff of an *acrid* odor. What could cause it?

5. Which might *exacerbate* each of these. . .

   YOUR BOYFRIEND (OR GIRLFRIEND) DUMPING YOU?

   A TEMPER TANTRUM?

   A HOSTAGE SITUATION?

   AN ARGUMENT?

   A HEADACHE?

Name_____

implausible

(adj) unbelievable; unreasonable; unlikely

1. Read the words in the list. What do their prefixes have in common with each other and with the symbol on Boomerang's shirt?

2. Circle words on the list that have a meaning close to *implausible*.

3. Finish these sentences:

_____
is an implausible hobby for a three-legged cat.

It's implausible that a rock music fanatic would stop

_____.

4. What do you imagine is the most *implausible* thing that could happen to you at school today?

implausible
    irregular
indivisible
    improbable
unfathomable
    nonsensical
illogical
    irreversible
inconceivable
    *illegible
immortal
    unstable
nonexistent
    discomfort

5. Write something in the box that demonstrates the meaning of the starred word on the list.

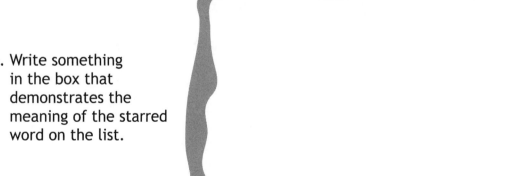

Name_____

fervor

(n) great enthusiasm; passion

apathy

(n) lack of emotion or interest

1. What are some signs of *fervor*? (Include some that are not shown in the cartoon.)

2. What are some signs of *apathy*? (Include some not shown in the cartoon.)

3. Name a person you know or a category of people that is . . .

APATHETIC ABOUT FOOTBALL	FERVENT ABOUT READING
FERVENT ABOUT BLOGGING	APATHETIC ABOUT POLITICS
APATHETIC ABOUT ROCK MUSIC	FERVENT ABOUT MOVIES

4. Finish the poems.

Apathetic Abby

The prom is 'round the corner
But Abby doesn't care.
She's got a case of apathy.
She'll only sit and stare.

She doesn't plan to go and dance
Though all her friends can't wait.
The prom is 'round the corner
Abby_____

Fervant Fred

Fred had racing fever yesterday.
Today he's on the hill
And fervent about skiing
_____

Tomorrow he'll have fervor
For music he can play,
Or _____or _____or_____
His passion changes every day.

Name_____

egotism *(adj)* an exaggerated sense of self-importance

1. How does the cartoon show *egotism*?

Which character (do you suppose) has the biggest *ego*?

2. What might be the effects of the display of *egotism* shown in the comic strip?

3. How can you tell that someone is *egotistic*? (Give three or more signs.)

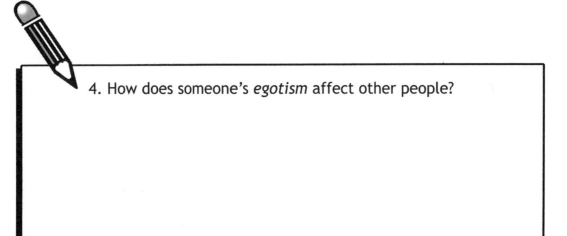

4. How does someone's *egotism* affect other people?

Name_____

92

alleviate
(v) relieve; lessen

1. Read the cartoon. What do you think Rosco is attempting to *alleviate*?

Will his attempts work?

> IT'S BEEN A SLOW WEEK IN THE PILFERING BUSINESS.

> SOMETIMES A RAT HAS TO MAKE DO!

2. Give a suggestion for something that could be done to *alleviate* each of the following.

- STRESS
- A HEADACHE
- POVERTY
- NERVOUSNESS
- GUILT
- HURT
- SHYNESS
- BOREDOM
- USE OF GASOLINE AND OIL

3. Finish the analogies by circling the best word for the blank.

investigate : _____ :: alleviate : burden

detective   crime   examine   ignore

satisfy : frustrate :: alleviate : _____

deviate   soothe   exacerbate   defer

4. Here's a way to remember the meaning of the word. Think of ALL the things Rosco might draw to *alleviate* his hunger. Write something for every letter of the word.

A_____ L_____ L_____ E_____ V_____ I_____ A_____ T_____ E_____

Name_____

truancy *(n)* act of skipping school

What's the connotation?
(What are all the things this word brings to your mind?)

What causes *truancy*?

What are some results of *truancy*?

What can be done to reduce *truancy*?

Name_____

content (CONtent)

(n) material inside something

content (conTENT)

(adj) feeling of satisfaction

1. How does the cartoon on the right demonstrate the meaning of *content* (conTENT)?

I JUST RETURNED FROM THE CHEESE CAPITAL OF THE WORLD. I *LOVED* IT!

2. Name ten things that could contain *content* or *contents* (CONtents).

3. Get together with a partner. Tell her or him:

   a. the one thing that most leaves you feeling *contented*

   b. the one thing that most leads to *discontent* for you

4. What do you suppose are the *contents* of Rosco Rat's trunk? Fill in the bubble above Rosco's head with a thought that uses both meanings of the word *content*.

Name_____

emulate

(v) to strive to equal or surpass—usually through imitation

1. Rosco can't resist *emulating* someone he admires (or envies). Whom could he be *emulating* with this move?

2. What are the results likely to be?

3. Describe five situations or people (without names) that are NOT wise to *emulate*.

   a.

   b.

   c.

   d.

   e.

4. Create a poster that gives advice about *emulating* others.

Name_____

debacle

(n) a disaster; a complete failure

1. Rosco's ski debut has not turned out so well. Get together with two other people and discuss what Rosco might have done to prevent this *debacle*. Write your ideas here:

2. For each letter of the word, write another word or phrase that could describe a *debacle*.

D
E
B
A
C
L
E

3. Find the meaning of the word fiasco. Tell how it relates to *debacle*.

4. What is the worst *debacle* you have witnessed or experienced?

How did you or another person get out of the *debacle*?

Name_____

catastrophic

(adj) greatly disastrous or unfortunate; utter failure

Here are ten CAT questions. Give a brief answer to each one.
You will probably need to consult your dictionary.

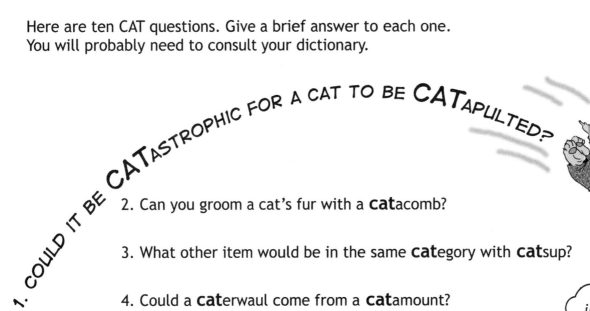

1. COULD IT BE **CAT**ASTROPHIC FOR A CAT TO BE **CAT**APULTED?

LOOK OUT BELOW!

2. Can you groom a cat's fur with a **cat**acomb?

3. What other item would be in the same **cat**egory with **cat**sup?

4. Could a **cat**erwaul come from a **cat**amount?

5. Who is sitting **cat**ty-corner from you right now?

6. What might cause **cat**calls at a basketball game?

7. What would happen if a **cat**amaran went over a **cat**aract?

8. Would you expect to study **cat**echisms or **cat**aclysms at a church?

9. Could a **cat**alyst do tricks on a **cat**walk?

10. What is the most recent **cat**ty remark you have made or heard?

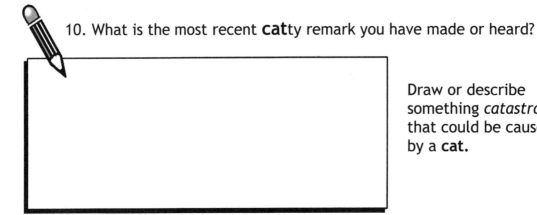

Draw or describe
something *catastrophic*
that could be caused
by a **cat.**

Name_____

encore

(n) a further performance

a. _____

b. _____

c. _____

d. _____

e. _____

f. _____

1. Here are some "happenings" from this book. Match the vocabulary words to the cartoons. Write one of these words on each of the lines:

   EXTRICATE   FAUX   UNDULATE   HISTRIONICS   PUGILIST   UNINHIBITED

2. Which of these (above) would you most like to see as an encore?

   Why?

3. What event or accomplishment in your life would you like to repeat as an *encore*?

Name_____

Put Your Vocabulary to Work!
Review and Assessment

Name _____ Date _____

1. If you could choose any legal and relatively safe escapade to carry out, what would it be?

2. Why might someone eschew clowns?

3. What is the root of these words?

COGNITION   COGENT

RECOGNIZE   INCOGNITO

What does the root mean?

4. J. J. turned in a faux research paper. Should the teacher applaud him or reprimand him?

5. Picture something that is illegible:

6. Which two of the following words are least likely to be connected to this illustration?

ACERBIC

PERIL

IRASCIBLE

PROHIBIT

CONCISE

GESTURE

ACRIMONY

REGALIA

FERVOR

7. In what situation or place do you feel most uninhibited?

8. Which of these is **least likely** to be concise?
a. a text message
b. a tweet
c. a message on a sign
d. a prescription for medicine
e. an autobiography

9. What word completes the analogy?

penchant : love : : _____ : loathe

aversion   debacle   lack   dilemma

10. A skier ignores a sign that says: "No aerial stunts allowed" and sails over a mound of snow to demonstrate a flying-helicopter trick in the air. Is she flouting or flaunting the rules?

11. Name two situations, events, or conditions that you think are best NOT to obstruct.

1.

2.

12. Is it a good idea to be in collusion with someone who is known to be a nefarious character? _____ Explain your answer.

13. Give an antonym for the word *restrain*.

14. Which sentence or sentences below use the word *negligible*, *negligent*, or *negligence* correctly?

A. THE NEGLIGIBLE AMOUNT OF FOOD IN THE ALLEY LEFT THE RAT RAVENOUS.

B. IT WAS NEGLIGIBLE OF YOU TO LEAVE THE LID OFF THE GARBAGE CAN.

C. YOUR NEGLIGENCE AT PUTTING AWAY FOOD HAS LED TO A PLETHORA OF RATS.

D. DON'T WORRY! THERE ARE ONLY A NEGLIGENT NUMBER OF RATS.

15. Which two words would NOT be applicable to the situation in the cartoon?

PAUCITY

PLETHORA

UBIQUITOUS

DIRE

NEGLIGIBLE

INORDINATE

16. How could Rosco Rat get extricated from the situation shown in the cartoon?

---

17. Pranksters prowled the neighborhood, breaking windows and letting air out of tires. Was this an illicit or an elicit activity?

18. What do you when you are overcome by monotony?

19. If you find a sycophant, what should you do with it?

    A. PLANT IT.

    B. OPERATE ON IT.

    C. SLICE IT.

    D. SING TO IT.

    E. ESCAPE FROM IT.

    F. MEMORIZE IT.

    G. MEASURE IT.

    H. GIVE IT A BATH.

20. Could you take a course in histrionics in your school?

21. Describe three examples of things you have seen that are synchronized or that you COULD synchronize.

    1.

    2.

    3.

22. When you put on your earphones to listen to a composition of sounds, would you prefer to listen to euphony or cacophony?

_____

Explain your answer.

23. What word completes the analogy?

    dire : _____ : : complicit : uninvolved

    extreme guilty culpable negligible

CHRONIC TRUANCY PROMOTES GOOD LEARNING

24. This sign was created to post in front of a middle school. What word or words could be replaced to fix the sign maker's blunder?

25. Which of the following activities are benign?

a. A mouse nibbles on crumbs at a city landfill.

b. Two friends wrestle carefully.

c. Several students taunt a lone student.

d. Ziggy sells answers to an upcoming science test.

e. Suzie creates a cartoon about characters who gossip.

f. Maizey writes and shares notes with gossip about classmates.

26. *The Daily Gazette* newspaper publishes damaging misinformation about a popular singer. Is this slander or libel?

27. What might cause chaos at a school assembly?

28. Name something that is in peril in your neighborhood, city, or country.

29. Where are you most likely to find regalia?

A. IN A POND

B. NEAR A KIDNEY

C. ON A QUEEN

D. UNDER A BRIDGE

E. COVERED WITH SAUCE

30. Every day, when a group of rats visits this garbage can, it is overflowing with juicy garbage. What deduction can you make as to why it looks like this today?

31. A strong, warm wind is pushing a forest fire rapidly toward a small western town. Is the town in imminent or eminent danger?

32. Name something about which you are ambivalent:

Tell why:

33. What might induce a building to vacillate and a bridge to undulate?

34. Circle the phrases that could describe the cartoon above.

RESTRAINED BEHAVIOR

UNABASHED GLUTTONY

ALLEVIATING HUNGER

ACUTE HUNGER

PROMINENT NOSE

SERIOUS GOURMAND

APATHETIC EATER

35. Amelia boards an airplane with her brother Mike. They sit across the aisle from a boy and girl who appear to be about the same ages as Amelia and Mike. The girl has a backpack that is identical to Amelia's. Is this most likely a coincidence, or clearly not a coincidence?

36. Give a synonym for *amend*.

37. What word completes the analogy?

_____ : senseless : : emulate : copy

insane   sensible   imitate   inane

38. Is a novice at reading likely to read a 400-page novel?

39. Which of the following sentences includes a malapropism?

a. When the floods came, our school had to be evaporated.

b. We also left the school one time when the incinerator exploded.

40. Would you expect to find a catamaran in a catacomb?

41. What is the meaning of the root of these words: *malodorous, dismal, malice,* and *malaise*?

42. A robber slinks behind a building in the dark, repeatedly watching over his shoulder. Is he behaving in a furtive manner or a futile manner?

43. Dionne is reluctant to climb into the car of *The Giant Dipper*, a very old wooden roller coaster. Is he loathe to board *The Giant DIpper* or loath to board it?

44. In which of these places or situations would you be most likely to find a pugilist?

    A. UNDER A TOENAIL

    B. MARCHING IN A PARADE

    C. ON A MENU

    D. IN A FLOWER ARRANGEMENT

    E. IN A BOXING RING

    F. PUTTING OUT A FIRE

    G. ON TOP OF A SALAD

45. Circle the word that does not have a similar meaning to the others.

    EGREGIOUS   PALTRY   HEINOUS

    GRIEVOUS   GROSS   FLAGRANT

46. How could you tell if your dog were in jeopardy?

47. What word or words would probably not describe the character in the cartoon above?

    AGHAST   CONTENT   INDOLENT

48. If a rat runs across a table in a fancy restaurant, is screaming and chaos inevitable or incongruous?

49. A therapist named Dr. Ann Ziaty just set up a business in our town. What is ironic about this?

50. If an innovation turned into a catastrophic debacle, what should you do with it?

    A. AUGMENT IT

    B. BUY IT

    C. GET AWAY FROM IT

    D. EMULATE IT

Escapade Record-Keeping Chart

Name_____

Directions: When you have completed the Escapade, write X over the number. When you are confident that you know the word well, write X in the *Yes!* column.

Esc	Word	YES!	Esc	Word	YES!	Esc	Word	YES!
1	escapade		31	furtive		61	piracy	
2	gourmand		32	inevitable		62	bona fide	
3	indolent		33	adjudicate		63	collaborate	
4	concise					64	novel, novice	
			34	collusion, complicit				
5	uninhibited		35	malapropism		65	induce	
6	pretense					66	dire	
7	culpable					67	philanthropy	
8	synchronize		36	sullen		68	nauseous	
			37	restrain				
9	unabashed		38	euphony, cacophony		69	pugilist	
10	virtuous, nefarious		39	augment		70	slander, libel	
			40	prominent		71	inane	
11	incognito					72	flaunt, flout	
12	undulate		41	deduction		73	metaphor	
13	monotony		42	exuberant		74	prohibit	
14	negligible, negligent		43	ambivalence				
			44	inordinate		75	aghast	
						76	postpone	
15	histrionics		45	elicit, illicit		77	meander	
16	dilemma		46	vacillate				
17	peril		47	faux		78	amend	
18	bamboozle		48	genius, prodigy		79	literacy	
19	incongruous		49	gesture, gesticulate				
						80	acrimony, acrid, acerbic, exacerbate	
20	eminent, imminent		50	futile				
			51	innovation				
21	eschew		52	obstruct		81	implausible	
22	egregious					82	fervor, apathy	
23	coincidence		53	chaos		83	egotism	
			54	jeopardize				
24	regalia		55	paucity, plethora		84	alleviate	
25	ubiquitous					85	truancy	
26	benign					86	content	
27	penchant		56	bane		87	emulate	
			57	obsequious				
28	irascible		58	irony		88	debacle	
29	extricate		59	obstinate		89	catastrophic	
30	acute, chronic		60	loathe, loath		90	encore	

106

Word List with Pronunciations

followed by Escapade Number (not page number)

acrimony (AK-rih-MOAN-ee) 80 *(n)* harshness of language or feeling

acerbic (ah-SUR-bik) 80 *(adj)* sour and biting in temper, mood, or tone

acrid (AK-rid) 80 *(adj)* sharp and biting

acute (uh-KUTE) 30 *(adj)* sharp; severe (but usually lasting a short time)

adjudicate (add-JUDE-ih-kate) 33 *(v)* to decide upon as a judge

aghast (uh-GAST) 75 *(adj)* filled with sudden shock, amazement, fright, or horror

alleviate (ah-LEVE-ee-ate) 84 *(v)* relieve; lessen

ambivalence (am-BIV-ah-lenss) 43 *(n)* the state of having opposing or conflicting feelings at the same time

amend (ah-MEND) 78 *(v)* improve; alter or rephrase

apathy (AP-uh-thee) 82 *(n)* lack of emotion or interest

augment (awg-MENT) 39 *(v)* make bigger; increase or add to

bamboozle (bam-BOOZ-ul) 18 *(v)* deceive by underhanded methods; con

bane (bane) 56 *(n)* cause of distress or suffering; poison

benign (bee-NINE) 26 *(adj)* gentle; not harmful; not malignant

bona fide (BONE-ah fide) 62 *(adj)* genuine; the real thing; done in good faith

cacophony (ka-KOF-oh-nee) 38 *(n)* harsh and unpleasant sound

catastrophic (KAT-ah-STROFF-ik) 89 *(adj)* greatly disastrous or unfortunate; utter failure

chaos (KAY-oss) 53 *(n)* complete disorder

chronic (KRAHN-ik) 30 *(adj)* ever present; lasting a long time

coincidence (koe-IN-si-denss) 23 *(n)* the occurrence of events that happen at the same time by accident but seem to have a connection

collaborate (koe-LAB-o-rate) 63 *(v)* work jointly with others

collusion (koe-LOO-shun) 34 *(n)* secret cooperation for deceit

complicit (kum-PLIS-it) 34 *(adj)* participating in guilt

concise (kon-SISSE) 4 *(adj)* brief and to the point; succinct

content (kon-TENT) 86 *(adj)* feeling of satisfaction

THE WORD OF THE DAY IS . . . UM . . . AH . . .

content (KON-tent) 86 *(n)* material inside something

culpable (CUL-puh-bul) 7 *(adj)* liable; responsible; at fault

debacle (dee-BOCK-ul) 88 *(n)* a disaster; a complete failure

deduction (dee-DUCK-shun) 41 *(n)* process of reaching a conclusion by reasoning from general principles; the conclusion that is reached by this process; *(n)* act of subtracting; the amount that is or may be subtracted

dilemma (dih-LEM-mah) 16 *(n)* undesirable choice; predicament

dire (dire) 66 *(adj)* extreme; nearly hopeless; causing fear or dread

egotism (EE-go-tism) 83 *(adj)* an exaggerated sense of self-importance

egregious (eh-GREE-jus) 22 *(adj)* notably bad

elicit (ee-LISS-it) 45 *(v)* bring out; draw forth

eminent (EM-in-ent) 20 *(adj)* outstanding; utmost; well-known and respected

emulate (EM-you-late) 87 *(v)* to strive to equal or surpass—usually through imitation

encore (AHN-kore) 90 *(n)* a further performance

escapade (ESS-kah-pade) 1 *(n)* an unconventional adventure

eschew (es-SHOE) 21 *(v)* avoid; shun

euphony (YOU-funny) 38 *(n)* pleasantly melodic sound

exacerbate (ex-AS-sir-bate) 80 *(v)* increase the bitterness or severity of something

I APPRECIATE THE MUSIC IN WORDS.

extricate (EX-trik-ate) 29 *(v)* set or get free from entanglement or difficulty

exuberant (EX-UBE-uhr-ant) 42 *(adj)* joyfully unrestrained

faux (foe) 47 *(adj)* false; fake

fervor (FIR-ver) 82 *(n)* great enthusiasm; passion

flaunt (flawnt) 72 *(v)* show off

flout (flout) 72 *(v)* disregard; treat with scorn

furtive (FIR-tiv) 31 *(adj)* stealthy; secretive

futile (FEW-tihl) 50 *(adj)* unsuccessful; useless

genius (JEEN-ee-us) 48 *(n)* a person with mental superiority; *(adj)* exceptionally brilliant

gesticulate (jes-TIK-you-late) 49 *(v)* make gestures, especially when speaking

gesture (JEST-ure) 49 *(n)* use of motions (especially limbs or body) to express ideas, emotions, or attitudes

gourmand (gore-MAUND) 2 *(n)* one who is excessively fond of eating and drinking good food

histrionics (HIS-tree-ON-iks) 15 *(n)* deliberate show of emotion for effect

illicit (ill-ISS-it) 45 *(adj)* unlawful

imminent (IM-min-ent) 20 *(adj)* just about to happen

implausible (im-PLAW-zih-bul) 81 *(adj)* unbelievable; unreasonable; unlikely

inane (in-AYNE) 71 *(adj)* silly or stupid

incognito (IN-cog-NEE-tow) 11, (adv) with one's identity concealed; unknown

incongruous (in-CON-grew-us) 19, *(adj)* out of place in a situation; inappropriate

indolent (IN-doe-lent) 3 *(adj)* averse to activity, effort, or movement; habitually lazy

induce (in-DEWSS) 65 *(v)* persuade; bring about

inevitable (in-EV-it-uh-bul) 32 *(adj)* unavoidable; certain

innovation (IN-no-VAY-shun) 51 *(n)* new idea or method

inordinate (in-ORD-in-uht) 44 *(adj)* unusual; excessive

irascible (ir-RASS-ih-bul) 28 *(adj)* easily angered; irritable

irony (EYE-run-ee) 58 *(n)* use of words to express the opposite of what is really meant; incongruity between actual and expected results of an event

jeopardize (JEP-urd-eyes) 54 *(v)* expose to loss or danger

libel (LIE-bul) 70 *(v)* to publish damaging misinformation about someone; *(n)* damaging misinformation about someone

literacy (LIT-ehr-uh-see) 79 *(n)* ability to read and write

loath (loath) 60 *(adj)* very reluctant

loathe (loathe) 60 *(v)* hate

loathing (LOW-thing) 60 *(n)* extreme disgust

loathsome (LOATH-sum) 60 *(adj)* repulsive

malapropism (MAL-ah-PRO-pizm) 35 *(n)* a humorous wrong use of a word (usually in place of another word that sounds similar)

meander (me-AN-dehr) 77 *(v)* follow a twisting route; wander slowly and aimlessly

metaphor (MET-uh-fore) 73 *(n)* a comparison of two unlike things; use of words to suggest a likeness between two things that are different

monotony (muh-NOT-uh-nee) 13 *(n)* tedious sameness

nauseous (NAW-zee-us) 68 *(adj)* causing disgust or a sick feeling in the stomach

nefarious (nah-FAIR-ee-us) 10 *(adj)* extremely wicked; evil

negligent (NEG-lih-jent) 14 *(adj)* habitually disregarding; carelessly leaving something unattended

negligible (NEG-lih-jah-bul) 14 *(adj)* so small and unimportant as to deserve little attention

novel (NAH-vuhl) 64 *(adj)* new or strange

novice (NAH-viss) 64 *(n)* someone untrained or inexperienced at a task or skill

obsequious (uhb-SEE-kwee-US) 57 *(adj)* excessively flattering or attentive; sucking up to

obstinate (OHB-steh-nut) 59 *(adj)* stubborn in sticking to an opinion, attitude, or course of action

obstruct (ohb-STRUKT) 52 *(v)* block; impede; slow down

paucity (PAW-sih-tee) 55 *(n)* shortage

penchant (PEN-chant) 27 *(n)* a strong taste or liking for something

peril (PARE-ihl) 17 *(n)* danger; exposure to the risk of being injured, destroyed, or lost

philanthropy (fil-LAN-thrah-pee) 67 *(n)* a desire to improve the well-being of humans; an active effort toward this improvement; a particular organization that promotes human welfare

piracy (PIE-ruh-see) 61 *(n)* robbery on the high seas; use of someone else's invention or property without permission

plethora (PLETH-or-uh) 55 *(n)* excess

postpone (post-PONE) 76 *(v)* put off until a later time

pretense (PRE-tenss) 6 *(n)* the act of pretending; a false appearance or action intended to deceive

prodigy (PROD-ih-jee) 48 *(n)* extraordinary accomplishment, person, or event; a child with great talent or skills

prohibit (pro-HIB-it) 74 *(v)* prevent by some authority

prominent (PROM-ih-nent) 40 *(adj)* noticeable; distinguished; standing out

pugilist (PEW-jih-list) 69 *(n)* a boxer

regalia (ruh-GALE-yuh) 24 *(n)* symbols of royalty; finery befitting a king or royal figure

restrain (ree-STRANE) 37 *(v)* limit or keep under control

slander (SLAN-der) 70 *(v)* to say false and damaging things about someone; *(n)* false and damaging things spoken about someone

sullen (SUH-len) 36 *(adj)* gloomily silent; dismal

synchronize (SINK-ruh-nize) 8 *(v)* occur at the same time; to operate in unison

truancy (TREW-an-see) 85 *(n)* act of skipping school

ubiquitous (you-BIH-kwit-us) 25 *(adj)* ever-present; seemingly everywhere

unabashed (UN-uh-BASHT) 9 *(adj)* not ashamed; not embarrassed; not surprised

undulate (UN-dew-LATE) 12 *(v)* rise and fall regularly; move in a flowing motion

uninhibited (UN-in-HIB-ih-ted) 5 *(adj)* unselfconscious; free from restraint

vacillate (VASS-ih-late) 46 *(v)* fluctuate; be indecisive

virtuous (VIRCH-you-us) 10 *(adj)* pure; morally good; righteous

110 ©Incentive Publications, Inc., Nashville, TN

Answer Keys

Note: Most of the questions or tasks within the Vocabulary Escapades are intended to be open-ended. For these, there will be many answers that are correct. Examine student answers to make sure they are reasonable and fitting in response to the task given. Encourage individual thinking, explanations, discussion, and comparison of responses. If an Escapade or task from a page is not shown here, you can expect varied answers. The answers given here are for those tasks which have a fairly clear right answer. Even for these, allow credit to students who give a different answer—if their idea can be justified.

Escapade #2 (pg 11)
4. Definitions of these three are very similar—but all different from gourmand. A *gourmand* enjoys ALL edible things, and is not discriminating the way the other three are; a *gourmet* is someone who is dedicated to the enjoyment of good food and drink; an *epicure* is someone with refined tastes, particularly for fine food and drink; a *bon vivant* is a person with refined taste, especially regarding food and drink.

Escapade #3 (pg 12)
5. root is *dol*

Escapade #4 (pg 13)
2. The actual proverbs here are a, b.

Escapade #5 (pg 14)
3. Label S: spontaneous, unwary, impetuous, daring, free-spirited; the other words are 0.

Escapade #7 (pg 16)
1. guilty

Escapade #8 (pg 17)
5. All can be labeled "in sync" except the third one: "persons of drastically different political viewpoints"

Escapade #9 (pg 18)
2. Connect: unbridled, haughty, egotistical, confident, brazen, audacious, flaunting, nonplussed.

Escapade #10 (pg 19)
4a. prank; 4b. lenient; 4c. indolent

Escapade #11 (pg 20)
4. Definitions: *cognition*: the mental process of knowing; *cogent*: convincing or believable because of a clear presentation; *recognize*: to show knowledge of; *incognizant*: lacking awareness or knowledge of; *cogitate*: to think about carefully

Escapade #12 (pg 21)
3. Definition of *fluctuate*: to vary irregularly

Escapade #13 (pg 22)
1. Circle: the dreary regularity of doing nothing.

Escapade #14 (pg 23)
4a. yes; 4b. yes; 4c. yes; 4d. no

Escapade #16 (pg 25)
4. A *quandary* is a state of uncertainty—a predicament from which it is hard to extricate oneself. A *dilemma* is very similar, but has the element of choice between two alternatives.

Escapade #17 (pg 26)
4. Definitions of the words (though students may arrive at definitions that are somewhat different): *perish*: to become destroyed; *perishable*: able to be destroyed; *imperil*: cause to be exposed to destruction; *perilous*: pertaining to exposure to destruction

Escapade #20 (pg 29)
4. All but the final sentence use the word correctly.

Escapade #22 (pg 31)
4. Circle: gross, flagrant, shocking, insufferable, notorious, heinous, grievous.

Escapade #23 (pg 32)
2. a, b, and e are clearly coincidental. (Students may argue that others are also.)

Escapade #24 (pg 33)
1. throne, crown, jewelry, robe;
3. Circle: costume party, parade, stage, closet, photograph, coronation, museum, history website, safe deposit box.

Escapade #26 (pg 35)
3a. benefits: good results
3b. benevolent: generous
3c. beneficiary: someone who is identified to receive something good
3d. benefactor: someone who gives something to someone
4. probably the first and last are benign

Escapade #27 (pg 36)
3. synonyms: fondness, relish, affinity, proclivity, and attraction; other words are antonyms

Escapade #28 (pg 37)
3. Circle: ornery, cantankerous, livid, cranky, snarls. Draw a box around: amiable, tranquil, generous, tolerant.

Escapade #29 (pg 38)
4. *Extract* means to remove—usually with some force.

Escapade #31 (pg 40)
3. Circle: a, b, and c.
4. Circle: public, forthright, aboveboard, brazen.

Escapade #32 (pg 41)
3. Circle: c, d.

Escapade #34 (pg 43)
2. seven; 3. Circle a, e.

Escapade #35 (pg 44)
1. Circle: abdominal-abominable; Comma-Comet; thesaurus-any dinosaur name; salted-assaulted;

psalm–palm;
century–sensory;
devised–advised;
altercation–alteration;
acrimony–matrimony;
granite–granted;
pigment–figment;
wows–vows;
evaporated–evacuated;
wildflowers–wildfire;
incarcerated–incinerated;
phantom–fathom;
2a. maladroit; 2b. malaise;
2c. malodorous ; 2d. dismal;
2e. maladjusted; 2f. malcontent;
2g. malfeasance; 2h. malice;
2i. malign; 2j. malediction;
2k. malevolent; 2l. malady

Escapade #40 (pg 49)
1. his nose;
3a. evident; 3b. obvious;
3c. conspicuous; 3d. protrusive;
3e. prestigious; 3f. jutting

Escapade #41 (pg 50)
2. no;
3. The Greens probably
have one cat.;
4. taxable income: $29,650

Escapade #42 (pg 51)
1. Cross out: exasperated,
lethargic, blue, restrained,
excavated.

Escapade #43 (pg 52)
3a. indecisive;
4b. ambivalent;
4c. certainty

Escapade #44 (pg 53)
3. Circle: moderate, inhibited,

reasonable, sensible.

Escapade #45 (pg 54)
4. a, d

Escapade #47 (pg 56)
2. five things

Escapade #48 (pg 57)
3. Zerah: yes to both;
Ruth: yes to both;
Akrit: yes to both;
Lexi: prodigy, yes;
genius: NEI

Escapade #51 (pg 60)
3. adjust

Escapade #56 (pg 65)
3a. poison, plague, or curse;
3b. annoyance, nuisance,
or affliction;
3c. curse, scourge, blight,
or plague;
3d. burden or plague;
3e. affliction, burden, curse,
nuisance, or annoyance

Escapade #57 (pg 66)
3. a, b

Escapade #58 (pg 67)
1. The irony is that the prize for
an essay on vegetarianism
includes hamburgers—a
nonvegetarian food.
2. The irony is that FaceBook is
hardly a place for privacy.
3. The irony is that, while writing
about the benefits of exercise,
Martin missed a chance for
physical exercise.

Escapade #59 (pg 68)
2. Circle: stubborn, inflexible,
recalcitrant, pigheaded,

insistent, obdurate,
headstrong.

Escapade #60 (pg 69)
1a. loathsome; 1b. loathe;
1c. loath; 1d. loathsome;
1e. loathing

Escapade #62 (pg 71)
3. c

Escapade #69 (pg 78)
2a. stealing; 2b. gloves;
2c. elegant

Escapade #73 (pg 82)
2a. chocolate syrup and her
smile; 2b. closet and garbage
dump; 2c. TWO metaphors:
1) Algebra and war;
2) end of the Algebra course
and a signed treaty

Escapade #80 (pg 89)
3. Circle: criticism,
condemnation, scolding.

Escapade #81 (pg 90)
1. They all mean "not."
2. Circle: improbable,
unfathomable, illogical,
and inconceivable.

Escapade #84 (pg 93)
3. first analogy: crime;
second analogy: exacerbate

Escapade #88 (pg 97)
3. *Fiasco* means a total
failure, especially one
that is humiliating; it is
a synonym for *debacle*.

Escapade #90 (pg 99)
1a. uninhibited; 1b. undulate;
1c. extricate; 1d. histrionics;
1e. faux; 1f. pugilist

Answers for Assessment, pages 100–105
AWV means that answers will vary. For these items, check to make sure
that student answers reflect understanding of the word meaning.

---

1. AWV
2. AWV
3. cog; to know
4. reprimand
5. AWV
6. concise, regalia (Students
may have good reasons to
choose other words.)
7. AWV
8. e
9. aversion
10. flouting
11. AWV
12. no; explanations will vary
13. AWV
14. A, C
15. paucity, negligible
16. AWV
17. illicit
18. AWV
19. E
20. no
21. AWV
22. AWV
23. negligible
24. AWV (Perhaps
replace "promotes"
with "inhibits")
25. a, e
26. slander
27. AWV
28. AWV
29. C
30. AWV
31. imminent
32. AWV
33. AWV
34. apathetic eater
35. coincidence
36. AWV
37. inane
38. no
39. a
40. no
41. bad
42. furtive
43. loath
44. E
45. paltry
46. AWV
47. content
48. inevitable
49. Her name
sounds like
"anxiety"—
which is
what therapists
may treat.
50. C